DELIRIOUS MIAMI

By Andrew Clum

Featuring
Cover Art by Erin Donahue
Photography by Qiazi Chen

"In republics founded by nomads, the assistance of foreigners is indispensable in all that concerns masonry."
-T.D. Allman, in reference to the City of the true Aleph

"The formula which shall haunt architecture forevermore... Technology + cardboard (or any other flimsy material) = reality"
-Rem Koolhaas, Delirious New York

2023 Edition Published in the United States of America by
Underwater Publishing & Media Group
25 SE 2nd Ave Miami, Florida 33131

ISBN: 979-8-9893520-0-5

CONTENTS

ACKNOWLEDGEMENTS........4

FOREWARD........6

INTRODUCTION........8

BEFORE THE DAYS OF SUB-DIVISIONS........14

SUBJUGATE, THEN INTEGRATE........20

GUAVANORMATIVITY AND THE TRUE ORIGINS OF THE SEALED BUILDING.30

COCONUTS AND CONCRETE: HOW TO MULTIPLY THE LAND........42

ECOLOGICAL SUCCESSION AND THE PIONEERING SPIRIT........54

INTERAMA: THE TRUEST MIAMI HAS (N)EVER BEEN........72

THE FIVE ASPIRATIONS OF MIAMI

    WEALTH (CONDOMINIUMS)........98

    PALACE (SINGLE FAMILY HOUSE)........104

    LEISURE (HOTEL)........108

    SPEED........118

    SPECTACLE........128

THE TYRANNY OF BEAUTY........136

FORM FOLLOWS FINANCE........144

APPENDIX: A SEMI-FICTIONAL CONCLUSION........150

THE STORY OF THE POOL, CONTINUED........154

ACKNOWLEDGEMENTS

I would like to start by thanking those who have stood by my side throughout my entire education, my parents Claire and Robert Clum.

Professor Jean-Francois Lejeune, my thesis advisor, has given me no small amount of direction and guidance in my research, from ensuring scholastic rigor to helping shape the themes that comprise this book. Furthermore, I would like to thank Professor Allan Shulman for his assistance in reviewing my work, which was extremely beneficial to the final product. Professors Lejeune and Shulman taught me not only through in-person reviews and critiques, but also through their extensive body of literature on the history of design and development in Miami. I will continue to learn from their written work long into the future.

I would also like to thank my literary influences; of course Rem Koolhaas for writing Delirious New York, a book which shaped contemporary architectural canon with irreverence and cunning wit. T.D. Allman has changed the way I see Miami, his books such as Miami, City of the Future, and the more recent Finding Florida are extensive and summarize thoroughly the themes authors have used to characterize Miami for over a century.

I would like to acknowledge Professor Elizabeth Plater-Zyberk for taking the time to answer interview questions and also for her enthusiastic support of my writing this book. Lizz, as she is called by her colleagues and students at the University of Miami School of Architecture, along with her husband, Andres Duany, have been instrumental in my education. Not only has their personal encouragement and mentorship been of great value, but also their contributions to the practice of architecture and urban design which have shaped the professions for the better.

I would like to thank Rocco Ceo not only for the knowledge he has imparted upon me about construction details, but also for his extensive knowledge of the tropical plants and gardens that are such an important part of Miami's character and identity.

Della Heiman, both for sharing her story of the Wynwood Yard and allowing me to interview her. Della helped me understand not only the dynamics of food service in Wynwood, but the development and curation of Miami culture itself.

Professor Jorge Trelles and Bernardo Rieveling, whose conversations on broader issues and challenges of Miami's future were the genesis of my decision to write this book.

I cannot make any acknowledgements in my undergraduate career without mentioning Christopher D'Amico, whose partnership on design projects has taught me more about architecture than anything else.

Qiazi Chen's photography has captured the new vibrancy of Miami like no other, he captures scenes with a lens that could usually only be expressed by an architect's hand.

Erin Donahue's extreme artistic intelligence has graced the cover that many will judge this book by. Her ability to incorporate the themes of the book into a single piece, playing off of Leonard Horowitz's color palette, is extraordinary.

Finally, I would like to thank my colleagues at the University of Miami School of Architecture, too numerous to name here, but many of whom have shaped this book through their encouragement, sharing, and personal support.

FOREWARD

WRITTEN BY
STEVEN FETT, ARCHITECT

Miami is often referred to as "Magic City." The story goes that this moniker was established by seasonal visitors who would remark how quickly (and therefore magically) the city developed from one year to the next. This periodic observation of place has been associated with Miami since its inception. Miami's history is told by the transient. It is a city largely built by others, for others. Miami has always presented itself as a place to be conquered rather than conformed to. J.E. Ingraham, who was Vice-President of the Florida East Coast Railroad, preferred to describe Miami as the "City of Eternal Youth," comprised of a population without fear of consequence as they inhabited the seemingly uninhabitable. This pioneer spirit has largely focused on land development with a repeating pattern of boom and bust. Fiscal cliffs follow frenzied patterns of overzealous investment optimism, often with mother nature at the controls, blowing her winds and leaving behind wreckage, only to be built up again, seemingly faster and faster.

In "Delirious Miami," a respectful tongue in cheek reference to Rem Koolhaus' seminal publication, "Delirious New York," Andrew Clum explores Miami's remarkable persistence and presents the City for what it is: an extraordinary work in progress. Clum weaves stories of historic happenstances alongside accounts of key figures who left indelible impacts on the City, all told in the context of Miami's unforgiving natural environment. Clum grew up in Boca Raton, just 45 minutes north of Miami, a city so culturally different it might as well have been as far as New York. A collection of youthful experiences cataloged a collection of postcard-like memories of Miami, but it would only be when Clum came to study architecture at the University of Miami that he would begin to unpack the "delirious" mythology. Upon graduation, he left Miami, only to return a year later, continuing his exploration of place through applied research, design and construction. Building in Miami gives one the perspective of a city that is simultaneously connected to its origins and its future. Clum entices the reader to indulge in the spectacle of "Delirious Miami" as he presents the unfinished story of Miami playfully, and positions the city as a global laboratory at the front line of environmental consequentialism.

INTRODUCTION

"It is difficult to plant a flag in a sponge."
- Joe Minicozzi

GEOLOGICAL PACT

The spirit of Miami has lied dormant for much of its geological history, bubbling quietly under the surface just as the waters of its freshwater aquifers have for eons. Miami rests upon oolitic limestone, coral rock that has been built up from the carcasses of sea-dwelling organisms, calcified over millions of years. The limestone is permeable and allows for waters of the aquifer to flow freely through it. An ideal city does the same with its people. Miami allows for people to flow through it easily.

It seems as though before humans inhabited the region, the Sun, the Sea and the Earth made a geological pact for Miami. The Earth and the Sea agreed to an even split, their compromise resulting in a peninsula formed from not-quite land and not-quite water. The sun, for its part, would gaze upon the region with harsh, unforgiving sunshine that would heat up the land and the water. Thus, the rich air would be heavy with heat and moisture, the land contending with but not quite overtaken by the sea. The sea, in turn, would be protected by the land. Not quite boiling away, but instead simmering and steaming, constantly replenished by summer rains. It is this pact that would pre-empt the city that would be established thousands of years later.

The end of the most recent ice age, nearly 10,000 years ago, brought with it rising seas as the northern ice sheets began to melt. Higher sea levels and a warmer globe brought a sub-tropical climate to the region. 5,000 years passed, and Lake Okeechobee was formed, and began to feed what is known today as the Everglades. The rising waters turned the Florida peninsula into a wetter environment, with lakes, rivers, and marshes. The plant life adapted, with new species to replace the existing species, which in turn had replaced those before them, all of whom were supported by the coral skeletons which pre-empted the land.

In Miami, the rule is this: the non-native is ever-present. The entire human history of Miami has been constantly re-written by the non-native. Miami is constantly being molded, like play-doh, pliable and ready for those who wish to come and make their mark. As T.D. Allman states in his groundbreaking book *Finding Florida*, which has inspired much of this introduction, "*Florida is the Play-Doh State. Take the goo, mold it to your dream. Then watch the dream ooze back into goo. People are constantly ruining Florida; Florida is constantly ruining them back. For at least 500 years that has been Florida's defining theme- whoever the protagonists are, whatever their dream is, whatever flag they wave.*"

SELF-INVENTION

In a quiet, still wilderness of the mid-1800s, its seems as though the sea once again made a deal with the sun. Upon the founding of the city, a metropolis would be conceived from the same spirit of western civilization as what Rem Koolhaas referred to as Manhattanism. In Miami, the Super-Tropical was born. Miamians have relentlessly fallen into the trap of comparing their city to Manhattan.

Those who call the City of Eternal Youth home do themselves a disservice when they compare their skyline to more well-established cities. Miami is self-referential. Miami's skyline is made from skyscrapers completely unlike those of Manhattan, which are cold and sharp like the air which bites at the buildings from all sides. Miami's buildings scrape a sky that is palpably different, hot and thick with vapor that rises from the earth. The air makes the buildings of Miami shimmer and vibrate, their forms simultaneously forged by the sun and

THOUGH THIS POSTCARD REPRESENTS MIAMI'S CHARACTER, NO SEEMINGLY NATURAL ELEMENT IS NATIVE. (FROM LEFT TO RIGHT) THE WHITE BEACH ON THE SEASHORE WAS ARTIFICIALLY EXCAVATED AND TRANSPORTED TO CREATE THIS BEACH. THE ORANGE WAS IMPORTED BY EUROPEANS FROM CHINA. FLAMINGOS ARE, LIKE THE WOMEN PICTURED NEXT TO THEM, JUST TOURISTS OF FLORIDA. COCONUT PALMS WERE IMPORTED BY FARMERS.

softened by the sticky warm air.

Though the metropolis has a spirit all its own and an identity deeply rooted in its physicality, the history of Miami is irrefutably linked to that of New York City.

UNAUTHORIZED SEQUEL

Why choose Delirious New York as a template for a critical analysis of the architecture and development of Miami? The spirit of 21st century Miami was undeniably conceived in 20th century New York. Many of Miami's founders left New York, never to return after being mesmerized by the fabricated landscape and invented culture. The parallels throughout Miami's development are consistent and unmistakable.

Miami led the world in the invention of an idealized landscape of the tropics. Seeing this trend, and being completely transfixed by it, Henry Flagler left his partnership with John D. Rockefeller at the Standard Oil Company. He unwittingly smuggled Manhattanism's counterpart, birthed from the same supernatural spirit, out of the city. Rem Koolhaas made the case in his seminal book, Delirious New York, that Manhattan was the arena for the terminal stage of western civilization. However, western civilization had already birthed another child of architecture alongside Manhattanism. That which grew up to be Manhattanism was the heir to the 20th century, but the bloodline that would be heir to the 21st century was already on a train south. Just over a century ago, Miami was conceived in another place. That which makes Miami is, paradoxically, that which is not from Miami. Thus, the most paradigmatic American city was born. Miami is set to take the stage as the next great city of western civilization.

Miami is non-native. Miami is youthful. Miami is delirious.

Miami will not replace New York, but upon close observation and examination of the city, it can be determined that Miami is, indeed, heir to the 21st century.

MANIFEST DESTINY

The reasons people came to American cities varied, but from this variety, a singular mentality emerges. Survey the prosperous land, establish yourself within it. The rules of engagement with the land have always been this simple. Subjugate, then thrive; this is the driving force in American mythology that not only governs people, but also plants, ideas, and architecture. This law of survival of the fittest has always been enough.

In the coming century, this will not suffice. Miami adds the next step. A fascination with nature, which leads to its subsequent integration with human habitation.

SUBJUGATE, THEN INTEGRATE.

The pioneer mentality is present in all who reside in Miami.

Miami is unique and distinctly American, in that its development was not powered primarily by imperial decree, nor by its own natural resources, nor was it founded by a collective of religious pilgrims. Instead, the story of Miami's development is one of manifest destiny. It is a story mostly of speculative individuals, from Ponce de Leon's voyage to the New World, to Della Heiman's project in Wynwood. The triumph of the individual and the vision that comes from real estate speculation deeply reflect tales of American individualism.

The ancestors of every Miamian embodied the pioneer mentality, from the aboriginals who crossed the land bridge through Alaska during the last ice age, to the colonial Europeans searching for a better life in the new lands, to the freed slaves who traversed the land to establish new communities, to immigrants today who seek economic and cultural opportunity. Miami's entire history is that of the pioneer. Those who developed Miami did so in the most American spirit possible. They faced a quiet, strange place that was foreign to them.

The dormant spirit of Miami is in the process of awakening. The City of Eternal Youth is no longer a sleepy getaway for residents of the American Northeast. The word Miami has come to represent much more than the agglomeration of connected neighborhoods that characterize a city proper. In just over a century, Miami has come to envelop a metropolis that extends one-hundredfold beyond its initial settlement. Powered by the forces of globalization, the name of the city has become distinguished, recognizable to billions. Miami has become the catch-all term for its metropolitan region. In Darwinian fashion, it has dominated all other established monikers. Bound physically by the Everglades to the West and the Atlantic Ocean to the East, Miami has spread itself all over the globe. In its short history, it has seen tremendous achievement as well as heart-wrenching lows. The city invokes fascination and disgust. Many newcomers feel both simultaneously. One thing remains constant: everyone has something to say about the city. Miami touches something within all who step foot on its soil, supported by the rock through which water flows.

BEFORE THE DAYS OF SUB-DIVISIONS

"Wrapped in the solitude of the centuries and bathed in the sunshine of the tropics, the vast summerland of which Miami is now the center lay enveloped in a long Rip Van Winkle sleep, "unknown and unloved." It was a land primeval. Its unromantic history was made by the few wanderers who came and went... They wanted none of it. That was before the day of sub-divisions."
-Victor Rainbolt, *The Town That Climate Built*

THE LEGACY OF THE SWINE

When Hernando De Soto landed on the Floridian peninsula in 1593, he and his crew were not the only non-natives aboard the ship. As part of their provisions, they brought with them 13 pigs. These pigs were bred, their offspring raised and traded with the natives. Of course, some escaped captivity and made off into the wilderness. In North America today, there are over six million feral swine. The swine, attributed to Desoto's original 13,[1] have wreaked havoc upon ecosystems up through Canada, far from the original spot of Desoto's landing. De Soto's expedition established a theme that would resurface more than 300 years later. Time and time again, a new transgressor would appear in the Miami region. If successful, this newcomer species quickly became part of the cutthroat food chain. Miami's history, long before it even had a name, was one of self-cannibalization. Self-cannibalization would permeate the character of Miami so much, from the city's beginning this would be its only solution to its problems. The only way for Miami to deal with its own incoherence and lack of identity is to reinvent. The city would reinvent itself so many times, that for the its entire history, if one left for ten years, upon returning they would be astonished with the development of the city.

FARCE OF YOUTH

Many schoolchildren in Florida are taught that Ponce de Leon was one of the first European explorers in the New World, and that he discovered Florida. It is told that he died while searching for a fountain of youth. Ponce de Leon was not doing any such thing.[2] When he met his end, it was not a result of searching for an elixir of life. Instead, Ponce de Leon was searching for something just as ancient and almost as elusive. Valuable land. Initially just an unknown page boy, he gained status after partaking on Christopher Columbus' second Atlantic crossing. Cunningly, he rose through the ranks of expeditioners and made a name for himself. This was despite a lack of familial ties in a time when such connections were of utmost importance. He was then given royal patents by the King of Spain to explore.

Ponce de Leon spent years establishing a settlement in Puerto Rico. He ruthlessly exploited the land and the natives, enslaving the inhabitants of the island and working them to death. His expectation was that by extracting as much production value out of the island as possible, he would be rewarded with the right to govern the island. Instead, Columbus' son was made governor, and Ponce de Leon was given the right to colonize Florida as consolation.[3] In 1521, Ponce organized an expedition to establish a colony in Florida.[4] This colony would, at long last, be land of his own. His task: conquer, stabilize, and squeeze profit from the land. Fully intending upon exploiting the natives as in his previously successful but unrewarded scheme, Ponce set sail for Florida. The natives he encountered did not surrender as easily as those in Puerto Rico, and Ponce was mortally wounded. Ponce was just the first casualty in a never-ending line of people who would stake everything they had on the promise of a slice of Florida's land.

VOID

Miami's presence in early American history is almost non-existent. Besides a few Native American tribes with small populations. Before and after DeSoto and Ponce de Leon arrived, South Florida's land was almost complete wilderness, devoid of human touch. After their defeat at the hands of unconquered America, the Miami region would remain almost completely unsettled until the 20th century.

The mouth of the Miami River served as a geographical link between the barrier islands of Biscayne Bay, the Everglades, and the coastal upland ridge. This was a strategic location where the Tequesta Aboriginals established a village. Following in Ponce's footsteps, conquistador Pedro Menendez de Aviles attempted to once again conquer the landscape, establishing a garrison and Jesuit mission that would fail as a result of fighting between the Spanish and the Natives.[5] The Tequesta, along with the small tribes of the Calusa, Mayaimi (who the city is named after), Jaega, and Ais, succumbed to European diseases shortly thereafter. Bernard Romans, an English surveyor, would describe the settlement of the area as only about 80 families, all of whom left for Havana in 1763. From then until the early 1800s, the land would be "unknown and unloved" by humankind.

SURVIVAL OF THE FITTEST AND HYPER-REVISION

As defeat at the hands of the American wilderness would thwart De Soto, De Leon, and Menendez de Aviles, the legacy of their efforts would instead be the themes of colonialization and import/export. Just the conquistadors' crews arrived with pigs and other non-native provisions to sustain them on their journey to the new world, Miami's first American agricultural settlers would also bring with them supplies from far-away lands. Citrus, bananas, and other fruits from around the world were brought to the area, in the hopes

THE FIRST ADVERTISEMENT FOR MIAMI LAND IN 1830 WAS PUBLISHED WHEN THE MIAMI AREA WAS ALMOST COMPLETELY UNINHABITED. THERE WERE ONLY 8 PRIVATE CLAIMS ON THE LAND IN THE ENTIRE MIAMI AREA AT THE TIME.

that the subtropical climate would sustain their production and exportation to the north. As early as 1830, these non-native species would be advertised as a feature of Miami real estate and would be forevermore a part of Miami's identity.

OUTPOST

John Sewell, a man employed by Henry Flagler who would later be responsible for the incorporation of Miami in 1896, recounted a story from his childhood that explains both how small and precocious the area of Miami was, even a century after the United States' founding.

"One afternoon in the fall of 1876 my father was reading a newspaper when all at once he began to laugh and called his brother, John, and told him that Henry Waterson of the Louisville Courier Journal wanted to know where in the hell was Dade County. It was the year of the Hayes and Tilden presidential election and there was a tie in the United States and a tie in Florida until they could hear from Dade County..." There is much scholarship on Florida's role in the Bush-Gore election, but not many know that there was previously a much closer presidential race that would be held up not by a state, but by a single outpost county. *"...My father explained to his brother that Dade County was the Everglades county of Florida and several hundred miles from a railroad and the only way to reach the county was to go by boat to Key West, then go in a small boat to Miami, the county seat. After waiting several weeks for the election returns to reach Tallahassee, with no avail, the governor sent out a courier to Miami. On arriving here the courier found that there had been an election and the returns were turned over to ex-Governor Gleason to mail. They found that Governor Gleason had gone out on a week's deer hunt and to look over some of his lands... They found him and he had put the returns in his pocket and forgotten to mail them. There were only twenty-eight votes cast in this election - and Dade County had held up a presidential election of the*

United States."[6]

This would not be the last time that the small outpost of Miami Dade County would punch above its weight, nor would it be the last time that the state saw itself in the middle of a national election scandal.

SUBJUGATE, THEN INTEGRATE

"The first state to be discovered, Florida has been the last to be developed."
-Victor Rainbolt, *The Town That Climate Built*

"The drying of swamp is where Florida begins, at least the part of Florida that we recognize, the southern part where the real estate is now priceless, the part that half the country thinks of as its final destination. Swamp is what preserved Florida for so long against the country's progress... the balance of Florida was separated from civilization by water, not an impassable and violent river, but a thin and inclusive sheet that covered its limestone bowl."
- John Rothchild, *Up for Grabs*

BARRIER TO ENTRY

Save for a few natural ridges and peat islands, almost all of 19th century Florida South of Orlando was inundated with water. Two thirds of the land mass of the state was designated "wet and unfit for cultivation" by the federal government. The land was so worthless, that the U.S. legislature decided to give 24 million acres of federal land to the State of Florida. The State, in turn, also had no idea what to do with the worthless land and decided that it would sell the land to any hastily construed venture that would offer to drain it. Even when the State gave them the land for free and financed part of the dredging, many private entrepreneurs who attempted to drain the land failed, once they ravaged the high ground of lumber and other assets.[1] At the same time that pioneers expanded westward throughout the 1800s, Miami remained protected from

EVERY FEW YEARS, A STORM WILL REMIND
MIAMI'S INHABITANTS THAT THEIR PLOTS
OF LAND ARE ACTUALLY PLOTS OF DRAINED
SWAMPLAND.

settlement. A relatively thin film of water and muck, just a few feet deep, would prove to be a sufficient barrier to the type of pioneering that was happening elsewhere.[2] No intrepid band of immigrants or farmers could push through the Everglades with axes and construct a home, establishing a homestead as was done in the rest of the continental United States. Only a wealthy entrepreneur who could afford a dredge would be able to claim the land that lay just beneath the water's surface.

DRAINAGE GONE AWRY

The State of Florida was desperate to hand off the water-soaked lands, and hand off they did. A Philadelphia native by the name of Hamilton Disston left Tallahassee in 1881 having purchased enough real estate to make him the single largest property holder in the United States overnight.[3] Almost instantly, he resold about half of his property to cover most of his $1 million debt for the original purchase of the land. With the remaining 2 million acres that he gained at almost no personal cost, he ordered 2 huge dredging machines to scrape the land and create a canal system. His official intention was to create agricultural land on which to produce sugar cane, efforts that would eventually fail, but this was not Disston's true motive. He opened Florida land sales offices in many major U.S. cities, and even in Europe. His project was the largest real estate gamble the State had ever seen.

Unfortunately, Disston was over-extended at the wrong time, and his grand scheme would come crashing down around him in the financial panic of 1893. John Rothchild would later participate in the creation of a mythology around Disston. Because he was financially insolvent, Rothchild claims, *"Disston committed suicide in Philadelphia. He shot himself as he lay in his bathtub, at least ending his life with a successful drainage there."* Though the irony of this demise added to the narrative, this is almost certainly false. Obituaries from the time all published that Disston died of a heart attack in his bed.

COLLINS' SUPER-BRIDGE, AT THE TIME THE LONGEST WOODEN BRIDGE IN THE WORLD, GAVE BIRTH TO NEW REAL ESTATE.

His heirs ended up selling the land off for even less than what he had paid for it. Another visionary ruined by his failure to subjugate Miami. Following this attempt, in 1898 there was a push for the drainage of a portion of the Everglades to the west of the newly incorporated City of Miami. The trustees of the Internal Improvement Fund entered into a contract with the Florida East Coast Drainage and Sugar Company for the sale of almost 800,000 acres of Everglades. This project also failed.

SWAMPLAND SUBJUGATED

John Collins was a wealthy Quaker, known nationally for his work on the forefront of fruit cultivation. Upon visiting Miami Beach, he saw potential in the sleepy island, and bought five miles of property along the coast. In 1907, he began his operations, cultivating avocado and mango trees. He then expanded into tomatoes, potatoes, and Cavendish bananas. Like Collins, all of these plants were not native to Miami, but they did well in the warm climate. Collin's investments in cultivation on Miami Beach proved to be unprofitable, and, at 74 years old, he sought out advice and investment from his children and their families. They told him they saw great potential for a seaside resort on Miami Beach. They agreed to financially support the dredging of a canal on the island in order to drain the land, and simultaneously to build a bridge across Biscayne Bay to connect the island of Miami Beach to the city of Miami on the mainland. Colllin's bridge began to make the two and a half mile stretch across the bay, making it the largest wooden bridge in the world at the time. People would come to the bay daily to check on the progress of the ambitious effort. With only a half mile to go, Collins and his business partners ran out of capital. Without the automotive connection to the island, Collins couldn't sell any of his land for a good price. Carl Fisher, an industrialist millionaire who had a winter home in Miami, was also a speculative individual. Fisher, who amassed his fortune from the production of automobile headlights, built the Lincoln

LINCOLN ROAD DURING THE CLEARING OF SWAMPLAND.

LINCOLN ROAD, ESTABLISHED LUXURY SHOPPING DISTRICT.

Highway from New York City to San Francisco and established the Indianapolis Speedway. He was well versed with the importance of the personal vehicle to Miami's development. Fisher agreed to back bonds for the bridge if he was granted land on Miami Beach. Fisher's dealings eventually found him with 300 acres of land on the island. Collins and Fisher would see the bridge finished, the land exploded in value. They had the marshy land on Miami Beach cleared. For the first time in Miami's history, someone had conquered this swamp. Like the coral that built up the oolitic limestone, Collins and Fisher built upon the efforts of the deceased before them. They were, for the moment, the first to break out above the water successfully. Much later, in 1928, Fisher would connect his real estate investment to those in the north by establishing the Dixie Highway, connecting Chicago to Miami. Fisher saw extreme returns on the initially valueless land he bought, but, like so many before him, his ending was not a happy one. One year after completing his Dixie Highway that would bring millions to Miami Beach, the financial crash of 1929 hit. Fisher would end up another name on a long list of Florida investors who got caught overextended, and his immense wealth was destroyed. He would die at age 65, his body rattled by his impoverished existence and alcoholism. Years later, one Miami Beach project in particular would take advantage of the cleared land and progress beyond a simple act of subjugation of nature.

SWAMPLAND INTEGRATED

During Miami's land boom of the 1920s, Lincoln Road achieved national recognition for its pleasant streetscape and fashionable stores. Luxury brands were tenants of Lincoln Road buildings for decades, and the street was the apex of Miami's high-end retail until the late 1940s. At this time, directly following World War II, many main street shopping districts across the nation were failing, losing to competition from large auto oriented projects which drew shoppers from entire regions. Many of the high-end retail stores relocated to luxury

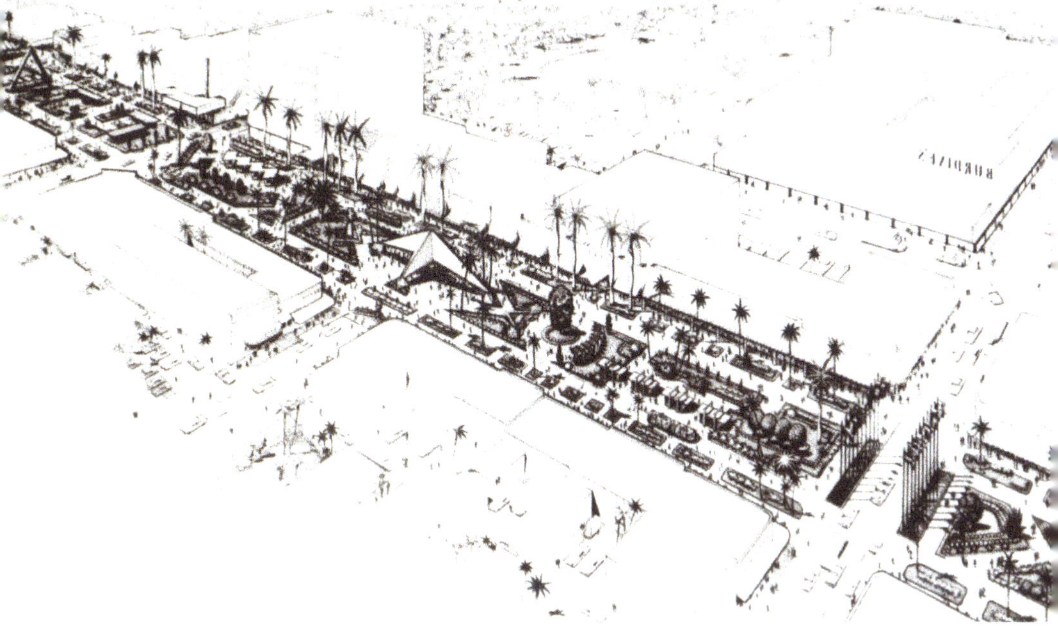

Lincoln Road, as proposed by Lapidus, Kornblath, Harle and Liebman in 1960.

Lincoln road as it is today.

hotels such as the Fontainebleau, which was designed by Miami's harbinger of the avante-garde, Morris Lapidus. Lapidus was not only an architect who was bringing a new aesthetic to Miami, but also a retail expert, who designed shopping concourses for many of his high-end projects. By the late 1950s, it was clear that Lincoln Road was losing the battle against other retail centers in the city.[4] A group of developers and landowners of Lincoln Road decided it was time to take action to bring Lincoln Road back into the spotlight, and who better than the man who designed projects that were beating them? Morris Lapidus was asked to create a new concept for Lincoln Road that would cut off the street to automotive traffic. In 1959, he presented his design to a room full of stakeholders - developers, property owners, retailers, and government officials who would be involved in the project. His plan designed Lincoln Road as a garden, with decorative fountains, public seating and street furniture, concrete shade pavillions, and exotic plants. These plants, as architect and historian Allan Shulman would note, made the space between the buildings of Lincoln Road seem more like a botanical garden than a street, and the low planters throughout the project were *"adorned with feather leafed palms from Madagascar, African cluster palms, dwarf date palms, Fiji fan palms, jewel orchids from Central America, hurricane lilies from Argentina, Abyssinian roses and Brazilian red sage."*

These exotic plants, replacing the swampland that existed barely 50 years beforehand, integrated nature back into the man-made landscape. It was fabricated, falsified, and disingenuous, but it didn't matter. The design was a celebration of the natural land which had been conquered. It was an idealistic construction, an integration not of the swampland that came before it, but of the idea of a tropical landscape that never had existed. This fabrication produced incredible results, abstracting the water of the Everglades into many pools and fountains which recirculated over 100,000 gallons of water.

FANTASTIC CONSUMERISM

This strip of invented nature, running directly down the center of the pedestrian road, contained many of Lapidus' designs for concrete pavillions, some designed for shade, others shamelessly acting as glass pavilions for exhibiting merchandise. They were simply another tactic for the retailers to take advantage of advertising potential. In his design, Lapidus did not recreate nature as a preserve, rather he took natural elements and integrated them into what was now the human landscape. Lincoln Road's fantastic design resulted not out of a desire to return to nature, but instead a market-driven, sensible design scheme. Lapidus himself would later state: *"I designed Lincoln Road for people – a car never bought anything."*

GUAVANORMATIVITY AND THE TRUE ORIGINS OF THE SEALED BUILDING[1]

"The United States Weather Bureau pays a man four thousand dollars a year to forecast the weather in Miami. This is a flagrant waste of the people's money."
-Victor Rainbolt, *The Town That Climate Built,* 1924

GUAVA

Just as Miami's first advertisement (see image on page 17) proclaimed the abundance of *"Banana and Lime Trees"* in Miami, the city has ever since lured the potential visitor with promises of the exotic. Exotic plants were the first example of such promises, and landscape has been central to Miami's self-referential narrative ever since. Guavanormativity can be defined as the importation, repackaging, and commodification of that which is non-native to Miami. Guavas seem to the casual observer as essential to Miami as white sand. Guava pastries can be found everywhere, from high-end bakeries to gas stations. In fact, the tree, which can be found in suburban backyards across the greater Miami area today, is not

Guava plant, drawn by Francisco Manuel Blanco.

native and was first imported from Central and South America in the mid-1800s.[2] Like the guava, every major plant that seems to give Miami its identity and allure henceforth has been imported from elsewhere. This extended beyond edible fruits to the entire landscaping aesthetic of the region.

NORMATIVITY

To the bourgeois European of the colonial era, the tropics were a source of exciting utopian illusions. Disregarding the violence and tragic spread of disease during the colonization of the new world, the Europeans found descriptions of the tropical landscape both titillating and fantastic. Often depicted as a garden of Eden, the European fixation with the tropical landscape was ironic. Though they had little trouble in the theater of war, European explorers most often met their demise in the New World when they positioned themselves against nature. As the extraction of commodities from the West was achievable by enslaving and killing the natives with superior firearms, the one thing that foreign conquerors could not dominate and capture was the tropical climate. Miami's climate and ecology are not to be combatted by the faint of heart. This is why, as T.D. Allman states in his book, Finding Florida, *"in general only one out of every ten invading species manages to survive once it reaches Florida. This is because for all species, including humans, Florida's most salient characteristic is its inhospitability."*[3]

After tropical plants were "discovered" by Europeans, often from the pacific islands and mainland China, they were extremely difficult to transport and cultivate back in the higher latitudes of the expeditioners' homeland.

TECHNOLOGICAL ADVANCEMENT

Though the colonial attempts to capture the fruits of the tropical regions began in the 1500s, it took centuries of technological change to allow for the Europeans to begin successfully cultivating exotic fruits. The orangery,

Banyans (top) planted by Dr. John Gifford in Coconut Grove and coconut trees at Key Biscayne (bottom) planted by William Matheson.

preceding fully glazed greenhouses, originated in renaissance Italy due to improvements in glass-making technology. The first orangeries were temporarily constructed in the winter, allowing for the southern sun to come through the structure, and for the heat to be trapped by the glass and stored within the thick stone walls of the main palace. Aristocrats could now grow tropical plants year-round at their garden palaces. As they became more advanced, orangeries began to incorporate stove fires and other technologies to keep a constant temperature. Inspired by the orangery constructed in 1617 at the Palace of the Louvre, aristocrats throughout Europe were delighted by the prospect of cultivating citrus trees. Once it became trendy for the rich, market forces and the growing demand for tropical fruits meant that wealthy merchants were now patronizing botanical research. The director of the Dutch East India Company, Georges Clifford, brought a banana plant to the famous Carl Linnaeus to study it. In 1736, Linnaeus was able to make a banana plant bloom, and produced the first recorded banana to be grown in Europe. It would be named Musa Paradisiaca, or fruit of paradise. Linnaeus speculated in his published works as to whether or not the banana was the forbidden fruit spoken of in the bible. Popular fascination with forbidden fruit would not stop there. Guavanormativity, or the re-localization of plants throughout colonial empires in general, was one aspect of globalization that had a role in the development of Miami, the Americas, and indeed the whole globe. Guavanormativity would intoxicate the world, and lead to the rise of the conditioned building as we know it today.

BREAKTHROUGH

In the late 1820s, naturalist Nathaniel Ward invented the Wardian case, a small portable enclosure that allowed for easier transportation of exotic plants whose humidity and temperature had to be kept constant. Ward's glass terrarium was a miniature prototype for a new wave of European greenhouse designs

THE WARDIAN CASE, UNINTENTIONED PROTOTYPE FOR PAXTON'S CRYSTAL PALACE.

THE CRYSTAL PALACE, A MODEL WHICH WOULD BE INVERTED BY THE TROPICAL SKYSCRAPER.

that would influence architecture forevermore. Joseph Paxton, an English gardener, was also fascinated with the banana plant. Knowing that bananas needed constant heat year-round to be artificially supported in Britain, Paxton developed a new architecture.

ARCHITECTURAL INTERPRETATION

Referring to Ward's invention, Paxton created large scale glass structures that allowed for tropical plants to be researched on a large scale. In 1832, Paxton's Chatworth conservatory stood as the largest iron and glass structure in existence. The structure was a new typology, one that represented both complete mastery over nature and devoted fascination with it. The drainage system of the building separated external and internal runoff, so that not only the air, but the water of the biome would not be influenced by the outside world. The most important revolution of Paxton's work was that the climate of the inside of the building was separated from the climate outside. By 1835, Paxton's building was a success, with one banana plant producing more than one hundred fruits. Paxton named the species after his patron, calling it Musa cavendishii, after his employer, William Cavendish. Bananas are now the world's fourth most important crop after rice, wheat, and corn. Over 100 billion bananas are consumed each year, and each one is almost certainly a descendant of the banana plant grown in Paxton's building in 1835. In a true testament to globalization and the monocultures that result from it, the Cavendish banana is the dominant banana species, with almost no alternatives in mass production globally. Though today we associate the banana leaf with the Caribbean, the banana plant had never existed within the Americas until Europeans brought it there.

Bananas became grown globally, spreading alongside colonialism across the global south and the new world. In the 1930s, fruit trading companies saw synergies between the tourism industry in the Caribbean and the

PHOTO BY VERNE O. WILLIAMS — Showing Town House, Dempsey-Vanderbilt and Roney Plaza Hotels

Air conditioned "ice cube trays" lining Collins Ave.

transportation of bananas. Ad campaigns depicted black Jamaicans as props within the broader narrative of the taming of the jungle. In fact, just the opposite was true. Bananas were not tamed from the Jamaican jungle; after hundreds of years of travel between the Asian Pacific and Europe, the banana plantations replaced the Jamaican jungle. Postage stamps, greeting cards, and other media were used to further this image, and romanticize the legacy of slavery that was housed in the banana fields. After banana wilt, or panama disease, killed off nearly all crops of the primary banana species in the 1950s, the world turned to a species that was almost completely immune to the fungus - the cavendish.[4] The memory of this monumental shift in production is preserved today; artificial banana flavorings are based on the 1950s variety of banana, and taste nothing like the bananas we consume.

THE SEALED BUILDING

Paxton was commissioned to design a building for the 1851 Great Exhibit for the Works of Industry of All Nations. Instead of clearing the site, his design called for the building, called the Crystal Palace, to be constructed over the park, trees and all. After the exhibition was completed, the Palace was relocated and expanded, the new version over a quarter mile long and over 160 feet high. The scale of the building was unprecedented, but was a fitting monument to the English obsession with tropical plants. In its first year, the number of visitors equaled the entire population of England at the time. Beyond an entire park for tropical plants, the Crystal Palace's program included a museum, and an orchestra space that seated 20,000. Summer activities were organized in winter, as the Palace's operators had control over the internal environment. The Crystal Palace changed the entire profession of architecture, the subject of heated debate on whether a building made of iron and glass could be considered real architecture. While architects of the day were debating amongst themselves, the greenhouse spread with colonialism just as rapidly as the banana. The problem Paxton originally solved with his greenhouse was recreating the tropical climate in temperate regions. Little did he know; 100 years later his greenhouse would become the prototype for just the opposite: recreating a temperate climate in the tropics. His development and popularization of the steel and glass enclosure would be reversed, and centuries later perfected as the ultimate built fortification against the natural elements: the air-conditioned, air-sealed building. This set the stage for enormous population growth in what was to become the world's tropical city, the previously unconquered climate of Miami was now conquered. With air conditioning, refuge was finally provided from the elements that the conquistadors could not fight. Miami's climate took 400 years to conquer, and now, Miami's skyline is populated with buildings that would be impossible without the structural technologies of glass and steel pioneered by Paxton. Furthermore, the airtight seal created as a defense against the external environment would become not only preferred, but required by law in modern American construction, and indeed, in construction around the world.

REFRIGERATION

One of the greatest lies ever told about Miami was that the climate is always temperate. Though the advertisements in Florida's great land boom of the 1920s may have boasted "balmy breezes" and "tropical waters", the truth of the matter was that for half of the year, Florida was consistently hot and humid. Not only did locals have to fight the temperature, but they also had to fight mosquitoes and other bugs that thrived in the hot, soupy air. After the mass migration that came with the 1920s land boom, many people found that they preferred to spend the colder half of the year in Miami, and the warmer half of the year in their homes up north. Miami could not be a fully functioning city if conditions were only hospitable for half of the year. In 1844, Floridian physician John Gorrie built a refrigerator to produce ice for cooling the air for yellow fever patients. Gorrie received the first U.S. patent for his method of electrically creating ice in 1851. This method, which had been designed but not executed by two previous inventors, was unique in its use of vapor as the cooling element. As the father of refrigeration and air conditioning, Gorrie's innovation may have been as important to Miami's development as Paxton's. Air conditioning had become popular by the 1930s but only in theaters or large stores. It would not be until the 60s that air conditioning would be available for domestic units like hotels and homes. By 1968, during the Republican National convention, Norman Mailer would pen his famous analysis of the air-conditioned buildings of Miami.

"...air conditioning: natural climate transmogrified by technological climate. They say that in Miami Beach where air conditioning is pushed to that icy point where women may wear fur coats over their diamonds in the tropics. For ten miles, from the Diplomat to the Di Lido, above Hallandale Beach Boulevard down to Lincoln Mall, all the white refrigerators stood, piles of white refrigerators six and eight and twelve stories high, twenty stories high, shaped like sugar cubes and ice-cube trays on edge...yes, for ten miles the hotels for the delegates stood on the beach side of Collins Avenue... all oases for technological man. Deep air conditioning down to 68 degrees, ice-palaces to chill the fevered brain- when the air conditioning worked."

But it wasn't just the buildings that were sealed and refrigerated at this point. By the late 1960s, half of all cars in Miami were air conditioned. Paxton's interpretation of the Wardian case had come full circle. Once again, the climate-sealed and conditioned bubble was portable, bringing motorists from one air conditioned building to another without having to break a sweat (unless, of course, the walk from the car was longer than 30 seconds).

Julia Tuttle, founding mother of Miami. Tuttle showed great prudence negotiating with Flagler. Instead of one giant plot of land, she sold him land in a checkerboard pattern, forcing him to develop infrastructure that would benefit the whole region.

Henry Flagler, founding father of Miami. Flagler left one of the most powerful companies in history once he became fascinated with Florida.

COCONUTS AND CONCRETE: HOW TO MULTIPLY THE LAND

THE ADOPTIVE FATHER OF MIAMI

Henry Flagler is considered the father of Miami. He, like so many others responsible for the character of Miami, was not born within 1,000 miles of the place. He never even lived in Miami. Instead, he was a non-native force that acted upon the city from afar.

Born in Hopewell, New York in 1830, Flagler moved to Ohio at age 14 to work in his uncle's store. He continued to learn and do business in the North, and after a failed attempt to start a salt-mining company in Michigan, returned to Ohio to work in the grain industry. During this time, he met a man named John D. Rockefeller, who had also been involved in the grain industry. In 1867, Rockefeller approached Flagler, looking for an investor for his new company, Standard Oil. Flagler's step-brother, Stephen Harkness, invested $100,000 on the condition that Flagler be a founding partner along with Rockefeller and Samuel Andrews. [1] After initial success of the Standard Oil Company, Flagler and his family moved to New York City. Standard Oil, capitalizing on Flagler's knowledge of distribution within the grain industry, ruthlessly controlled shipping rates. As the rail lines were fiercely competitive for traffic, Standard Oil leaned upon the rail operating companies to recieve preferential treatment. As the biggest customer of rail companies, Standard Oil formed a cartel to exorbitantly increase shipping prices, and then muscled into an exclusive

50% discount on shipping costs. By 1880, Standard Oil was well on its way to becoming one of the most powerful companies in history. During this time, Flagler's first wife fell ill, and on the advice of their physician, the family moved to Jacksonville, Florida. When his first wife passed in 1881, Flagler was already intoxicated by the southern sun. Instead of returning to New York, he left his active role at Standard Oil in 1882.[2] Flagler developed the Ponce de Leon Hotel, which opened in St. Augustine in 1888. This hotel was more aptly named than Flagler could have predicted. Like Ponce, he was a conqueror who, after immense success elsewhere, would lose his immense fortune in the pursuit of developing Florida land with enormous potential.

In 1892, Flagler acquired the railroads to Daytona and built the Hotel Ormond. In 1894, he finished his railroad to West Palm Beach, and built the hotels Royal Poinciana and, years later, the Breakers.[3] Flagler, as he built his hotels like pearls on the string of his railroad lines, demonstrated his understanding of two fundamental principles of large scale development: anchors and phasing. Flagler's vision for the coast of Florida was to create a world's playground. He wanted to invent a tropical paradise that did not yet exist. Miami Beach's original settlers who preceded Collins and Fisher had acquired their land by planting coconut palms in the 1870s, before Flagler's influence reached the city. They were given land along the beach by the U.S. Government in payment for introducing coconut growing. They took boats South and, after loading up with coconuts as cargo, they sailed to the Miami coast. Once they arrived, they would anchor offshore and send men to the beach in a smaller boat, armed with a shovel and a bundle of coconuts. The men would then tie themselves up with rope in a straight line, forty or fifty feet apart. They would then head up the beach and plant another row of coconuts. The trees grew, and the settlers were then granted the land.[4] Flagler noticed this trend of people planting non-native coconut trees along the southern Florida coast. He decreed that these coconut palms be planted everywhere.[5] By doing so, he popularized the trend of the real estate developer's fabrication of nature in South Florida. These coconut palms, non-native biological invaders, were advertised in order to attract non-native people.

THE ADOPTIVE MOTHER OF MIAMI

Flagler was already discussing the possibility of bringing his railroad line down to Miami with Julia Tuttle, in exchange for her land, when the great freeze of 1894 hit.[6] Tuttle had been pursuing a railroad connection for years, and they finally struck a deal. In the wake of the disastrous frost that ruined much of the Florida agriculture industry, Tuttle and Flagler set up a PR stunt, through which she sent him and his wife a bouquet of fresh orange blossoms. Unlike those just 70 miles north, the orange blossoms that came from Miami had survived untouched by the frost. This tropical version of an olive branch was accepted.[7] Immediately, Flagler got to work extending his railroad down to Miami, and in 1896 sent down two of his railroad employees, brothers E.G. and John Sewell. Tuttle, unlike any of Miami's other founders, actually saw Miami as a new great American City. Of all Flagler's enthusiasm for his railroad, Miami to him was just another stop along the way to Key West. When he laid out the infrastructure for the city, he built expecting about eight thousand citizens. He paved narrow streets with narrow side-walks, never thinking that Miami would amount to much more than the backstage of the set as the supporting cast of his Royal Palm Hotel. By contrast, Tuttle would predict in 1896, half a century in advance, that "Miami will become the great center of South American trade."

HENCHMEN

The Sewell brothers, dispatched by Flagler, arrived and immediately began the process of incorporating Miami into an official city. Miami, with a population of just 300 people,[8] was miniscule compared to the major cities in the United

States. At this time in the mid-1890s, Chicago, with a population of over one million, was constructing the first skyline of skyscrapers in the world. Miami was nothing in comparison. John Sewell's memoirs regarding his plans to set up shop in the downtown give a sense of how far behind Miami's development was from America's major cities.

"When I first came here…I made up my mind right there and then to go into the shoe business. I went out and looked up Harry Tuttle to find out what I could rent from his mother that would do for a shoe store. He told me that his mother had been thinking of cutting off two stores from the rear end of the Miami Hotel dining room, facing them on avenue D, as the dining room was too large and they were building a mechanic's dining room east of the other the same size. So that left the guest dining room about forty feet too long. I told him to go and see his mother at once and tell her that I would take both stores, if she would make me a price on them, and put a shoe store in one and a drug store in the other, and to let me know at once. In less than half an hour Harry was back and said that his mother would cut off the two stores, each 20x34 feet, and rent them to me for $25.00 each per month, and would lease them to me for one year at that price. I told him to go to work at once and I would sign the lease and pay the rent."[9]

This was the state of the city in 1896. Upon arriving in the heart of Miami, cash in hand, one could simply ask to cut off a piece of the wood structure hotel, close up the sides with wood planks, orient it to the street, and then begin to do business out of the Frankensteined structure. Within one year of arriving, John Sewell had incorporated the city and rigged the first electoral ballot to include only "Flagler men."[10] Flagler's railroad interest had been quickly mounting in force, with some even suggesting that upon incorporation, the city be named not Miami, but "Flagler."[11]

Aerial photograph of the Royal Palm Hotel.

Grounds of the Royal Palm Hotel.

The legacy of Flagler's decree: hot, itchy public space

AGENDA: TALL PALMS, WHITE SAND, AND GREEN GRASS

After establishing a political body to govern the city, John Sewell got to work on developing Flagler's properties. Within one year of Miami's establishment, Flagler had already unleashed his agenda of tall palms, white sand, and green grass. He set about establishing his own hotel, called the Royal Palm, having John Sewell handle much of the development work. While working on clearing land for the Royal Palm Hotel, Sewell directly recounts this agenda that would be part of Miami's development forevermore.

"In this year of 1897 I did big business in street paving, grading, and filling. In addition to my regular rock pits... I blasted off four feet of solid rock in what is known as Royal Palm Park... We also received ten carloads of sand from a pit north of West Palm Beach every day... I would unload my train load of sand every night, keep moving my track north as it was needed... Also I had a hole blasted and cleaned out every twenty-five feet for coconut trees, which were brought here on lighters from Elliott's Key...I also had over two hundred negroes on this work, while Mr. McCarthy, one of the garden foremen, worked about fifty white men with wheelbarrows, spreading the sand over the park. Before blasting the rock off the park, I sent men over and scraped all of the black dirt off the rock and put it in piles. Then, after the gardeners spread the foot of sand they would spread about two inches of this black dirt. Then they planted the grass for the lawn. In the winter of 1898 we had a beautiful coconut grove and lawn where in the winter before we had nothing but a scrub and rock bluff. Also had a beautiful boulevard with a stone wall built out in the bay around the entire hotel grounds so as to give us an even shore line. All of this work was paid for by Mr. H.M. Flagler..."[12]

This method of taking the natural land, which Sewell refers to as *"nothing but scrub and rock bluff"*, and grafting an artificial landscape of grass, sand, and palms, continues into the present. Today, one can visit many of Miami's public spaces and experience for themselves the unnecessary discomfort that comes from standing on itchy St. Augustine grass, vulnerable to the beating rays of the hot subtropical sun under palm trees which provide no real shade. But the artificial landscape was never meant to make practical sense. Instead, it was mandated by a man who had not grown up in the environment and directed by men who were no more familiar with the native ecology. The pursuit of an idealized representation of tropical paradise has mattered more than the paradise itself for over a century. When dynamiting away at the limestone, Sewell also discovered that the powdered oolitic rock had cementitious properties. It was then used as a crude method of paving the streets of Miami until the 1910s. The rock powder was laid over a piped and leveled road subsurface, and then sprayed with water in order to calcify and harden over. [13]

ASSURED AUTOMOTIVE RULE

Sewell's use of powdered oolitic limestone as roadway cement was not confined to Flagler's private properties. After being appointed to a position on the Dade County board of commissioners for his experience in paving, he oversaw the construction of a road from Miami to West Palm Beach.[14] Though he was a "Flagler Man," automotive roads did not seem like a threat at the time to the locomotive industry.

LIMESTONE: FUNDAMENTAL LOCAL BUILDING MATERIAL

Though his building methods were rudimentary, John Sewell successfully incorporated locally sourced oolitic limestone, at that time referred to by locals as "Miami Stone," into both infrastructure and buildings. He made sure it was used in all of the civic buildings constructed by the city and the county. Sewell was so interested in using the material that he traveled to Washington, D.C. to try and have the federal government specify the material in the construction of the local post office. However, he could not convince the supervising architect, who instead selected a stone quarried in Indiana. Even his own house, constructed in 1918, was made from the locally sourced oolitic limestone, its walls 18 inches thick consisting of both solid stone and cement.

THE CITY OF ETERNAL YOUTH: THE END OF A 500 YEAR-LONG CHASE

Ponce de Leon's pursuit of eternal youth may have been a myth, but his efforts to colonialize and develop the Everglades were very real. Ponce de Leon's conquering spirit had stuck in the mud for over 300 years. Flagler, in dredging the mud of southern Florida to fulfill his dream of connecting Key West with New York City, unearthed this spirit and let it loose on the City of Miami.

Born out of the unconscious partnership between two conquerors separated by hundreds of years, this trope is lived out unconsciously by the drug dealers, truckers, immigrants, entrepreneurs, models, and real estate developers today. Miami's lifeblood has been the same throughout time:

Take the land, raise it above the water, and conquer it. Integrate your own non-native presence with the land. Become transfixed by the place and fabricate nature within the unnatural environment.

SEMI-CONSCIOUS PROPHECY

Seven years after Henry Flagler's passing, J.E. Ingraham, Vice-President of Flagler's Florida East Coast Railroad, made a speech before the Women's Club of Miami in 1920. This speech would nullify Miami's most popular nickname, "The Magic City", and express the more appropriate nickname for Miami: The City of Eternal Youth.

J.E. Ingraham's Prophecy for The City of Eternal Youth

Paradise Lost

"...the orange industry had been the chief industry of the State and had been growing year by ye
Trucking, general farming, dairying and stock raising were in their infancy. The first of the gre
freezes occurred on the 24th of December, 1894, very seriously injuring the orange groves to wh
was then known as the orange belt in the northern and central part of Florida, and it seemed
a time to be a disaster impossible to overcome for faith in Florida and confidence in its future w
materially shaken."

Maintaining Investor Confidence

"In 1896, immediately after the freeze, Mr. Flagler extended his railroad from West Palm Beach
Miami and established the town of Miami, and his action had much to do with restoring confiden
in the State, because other interests realized that if Mr. Flagler had not lost faith in the future
Florida with all of the millions involved in his investments, that they could also afford to go ahe
and rehabilitate the interests dependent upon them and they too helped the people of Florida
establish new industries and to develop a great many hitherto unknown or neglected resource
thus accomplishing a tremendous thing for the upbuilding of the State.

Buying The Dip

The second freeze occurred on February 7, 1895, and was far more serious than the first one becau
it came at a period when trees were in bloom, full of sap and therefore exceptionally susceptib
This caused the destruction of the greater part of the citrus groves of Florida that were left or h
recuperated from the former freeze, the pineries on the Indian River and the trucking industry whi
had been established in the southern part of the State. At this time, too, great disaster seem
imminent, but Mr. Flagler loaned large sums of money at low rates of interest to the people alo
the southeast coast of Florida to help them re-establish trucking permanently in the southea
counties."

Exponential Returns

"In 1896, ten years after the construction of the Ponce de Leon and Alcazar Hotels in St. Augustin
and the year in which the Florida East Coast Railroad was extended to Miami, the total value
the State for taxes of the counties through which the main line of the Florida East Coast Railroa
then ran, consisting of Duval, St. Johns, Putnam, Volusia, Brevard, and Dade was approximate
$23,000,000. In 1919 the total value of this same territory from Duval to Key West, including Monro
County, was $108,833,4256..."

City of Eternal Youth

"At the last interview I had with him... he [Flagler] was stretched on his bed in his home at Pal
Beach, pale with suffering, but thinking about the people and things of the East Coast of Florida
Then turning and putting his hand in mine, he said: 'Tell me of Miami. When were you there?' I sai
'I was there yesterday and the day before, just came from there this evening.' He said, 'What a
they doing?' I told him of things of interest to him and said 'It truly is a magic city.' 'No', he said, 'Yo
are mistaken. It is not a magic city, that is a misnomer. I look upon Miami as a city of Eternal Yout
Those men and women are like girls and boys who have never known fear. They do not know wh
it is to be afraid.'

ECOLOGICAL SUCCESSION AND THE PIONEERING SPIRIT

"In republics founded by nomads, the assistance of foreigners is indispensable in all that concerns masonry."
-T.D. Allman, in reference to the City of the true Aleph

PERMEABILITY

Miami champions the pioneering spirit. Just like the limestone upon which the city sits, the cultural ecology is both strong and permeable. Cultural permeability is an important aspect to the success of Miami, as the procurement of outside talent is key to any successful city. In 1895, George Merrick was brought to the Miami area as a young man. His father, a pastor, made the decision to bring the family down to Florida during a terrible winter storm in the northeast. Non-native settlers from New England, the Merricks came to the land to plant non-native fruits from South America. Would anything else make sense in this delirious land where ideas and people flow as freely as water through the limestone within the ground? George Merrick, a child when he and his family first moved to Miami, would in his adulthood found the suburb-city of Coral Gables, and retroactively create the duality that will define development and real estate opportunity forevermore.

THE URBAN PIONEER

George Merrick's Grandfather, (Henry) H.G.G. Fink, was an urban developer. A preacher and magic oil salesman, Fink was a charismatic and entrepreneuring carpetbagger who encouraged the Merrick family to descend upon Miami and buy land in the downtown. [1]

THE RURAL PIONEER

George Merrick's father, Solomon Merrick, was a quiet and serious man. He, like his father-in-law, was a preacher, but far from the snake oil selling type.[2] Solomon agreed to move the family down to Miami, as the tropical heat offered promise of cure to his failing health. Solomon disregarded comments that life was too hard in the backcountry of the Everglades and ignored his father-in-law's advice that he would be well-advised to purchase land in the already settled downtown. He decided to stick it out and buy land outside of the city to make his money from farming citrus trees. Essential to the pioneer mentality and the spirit of rural development, Miami is built upon the act of homesteading. Homesteading was enabled by the Homesteading Act of 1862 and granted land to U.S. settlers of undeveloped land who were willing to farm and develop it.[3] This was the legal mechanism through which South Beach was colonized through the importation and planting of coconut trees. Inland and Westward, however, would be largely cut off from homesteaders until the land was drained and cleared. Once Flagler connected his railroad to Miami, settlers were able to charge southward, not on wagon trains as the settlers of the west had traveled, but in the comfort of a train car. Homesteaders caught "Miami Fever" the instant the land was opened to them.

When the Merrick family first arrived, George's father dreamed of planting citrus trees. Just a few homesteads away, John Douglas and Potter Brothers' groves were prominent examples of grapefruit pioneers who made fortunes off cultivating the exotic fruit.[4]

MERRICK'S CROWNING ACHIEVEMENT, THE BILTMORE HOTEL. PHOTOGRAPH BY QIAZI CHEN.

CORAL GABLES WAS NAMED AFTER THIS HOME, BUILT FROM THE OOLITIC LIMESTONE OF THE MERRICK HOMESTEAD.

Before they had the money to invest in the expense of farming grapefruit, the Merricks settled for harvesting guava. Once the Merricks sold their crops of guava and saved enough money to invest in the higher yielding grapefruits, George and his father's laborers had to clear the ground by hand, ground which was chock-full of oolitic limestone. The rock George Merrick cleared would later be used to build the Merrick's home. The limestone that was uncovered and reused by the Merrick family eventually gave birth to the name of the city George would later establish, Coral Gables.[5] He also worked on road crews, clearing rock with pick and mattock, paving what is today Coral Way. The Merrick Family endured the hardships that came with the way of the rural pioneer. Arva Moore Parks would recount George Merrick's tale from one storm in particular.

"All the land between the "reefs," including most of the homesteaders' cabins, flooded. Road became impassible... No matter how bad the conditions were outside, they were worse inside their "Ark," as George called it. First the glade disappeared, along with their vegetables, under as much as six feet of water. The overflowing water then began moving toward their cabin. As the water rose, the family removed boards from the barn and nailed them to the cabin floor to raise the level against the flood. Then there were the roaches. They, plus a myriad of other insects, sought refuge inside the house. George wrote that the more they killed, the more the roaches seemed to reappear, as if raining from the skies. The frogs were no less disconcerting. "There was something horrifying in the clamor that unceasingly enveloped the cabin," George wrote. "The din was as if every rain drop, as ceaselessly they fell, gave birth to a new voice; a new croak, gurgle, gurk, grackle, and shriek." Adding to the noise was the loud bellowing of the alligators that swam in from the Everglades to devour stranded rabbits and snakes."[6]

THE SUB-URBAN PIONEER IN THE POLYCENTRIC METROPOLIS

George Merrick was a blend of his grandfather and father, creating a suburban paradise that co-opted nature first by conquering it, then by integrating it. George Merrick, after observing his grandfather's skill in the arena of the urban pioneer, and participating in his father's rural lifestyle, decided to use both sides of the spectrum to create an integral piece of the Miami tapestry. Part of the "Garden Cities" planning movement, Coral Gables was densely landscaped, and featured many examples of imported architecture within its fabricated tropical setting. Australian pines, gumbo limbo trees from Madagascar, Solomon Merrick's guavas, and other flora just as exotic characterized the landscape. The imported architecture consisted mainly of a Mediterranean Revival theme, but was also populated with international villages themed with Chinese, French, English, and Dutch-South African architectures.[7] Merrick's Coral Gables was just one of the dozens of other cities and neighborhoods that sprouted up in the region. Miami, as the paradigmatic 21st century metropolis, is polycentric from its very beginning. The shallow marshy waters that barricaded the landscape drove developments like Coral Gables, downtown Miami, and Miami Beach to all come into being simultaneously.

ECOLOGICAL SUCCESSION IN CITIES

The more developed downtowns in Miami, and in every metropolis, are characterized by success. By definition, they are the places where the success compounds. With more amenities, more activity, and more business opportunity, the core of development in a city has the highest land prices because it houses the highest amount of desire per square foot. However, for the entrepreneur, this landscape is not always the most hospitable. Municipalities seek to maintain their success, so they adopt restrictive codes and legal policies. These policies usually require an army of lawyers and compliance experts, and millions must be spent just to build something without breaking the law in Downtown Miami today. This type of downtown environment, though by definition successful, can stifle innovation and creativity though a regulatory environment that creates a barrier to those who would like to create positive change without spending millions of dollars. Though this amount of bureaucracy may seem like irrational overreach, municipalities must act to preserve quality in the areas that are most desirable. These important areas are vulnerable to overspeculation and, if development goes unchecked for quality, their value can be squandered within a single generation.

The land within cities undergoes succession just as land within nature does. Ecological succession is the concept that in nature, barren land may eventually gain biodiversity and complexity, leading to what is called a climax community. Through ecological succession, a given area of barren rock may eventually become a forest of hundred-foot tall trees. This process is classified into primary succession and secondary succession. Primary succession is the process of pioneer species, such as hearty plants or lichens that break down the bare rock, and, after they grow and die, help to create a layer of more nutrient-dense soil. This process can repeat itself multiple times before secondary succession takes place. Secondary succession is the process where an area is re-colonized, and pioneer species are disturbed and often killed by a natural event or an invading species. The new species takes advantage of the more fertile soil that it requires to succeed. Given enough time and the absence of another natural disaster or colonization event, the area will develop into a more diverse environment. (see illustration on page 57)

DIET

1960s zoning laws in the United States were a response to obese buildings. Zoning laws were a kind of governmental enforcement of building fitness. The laws became necessary as the ability to engorge buildings was technologically enabled, and the financial incentives to build obese buildings were too tempting. An American city, then, was seen as incomplete if it did not have a clearly prescribed zoning diet. Miami, the city of eternal youth, would not be caught dead without a world-class diet plan.

ANOREXIA

Miami, like many cities, fell into the trap of too stringent a diet. Cities became self-conscious in the 20th century, to an unhealthy extent. So fearful of bad buildings, crime, and complete urban failure, local governments decided that every aspect of development must be codified. Site function, density, design, you name it, there was a law that applied to it. By the 1980s, cities across the country were starving themselves to death with their zoning codes. In 1981, urban designers and Miami transplants Elizabeth Plater-Zyberk and Andres Duany led the national conversation, directing urban leaders and planners to look in the mirror and admit it - they were addicted to zoning. It is fitting that Miami, in all its self-absorption, would have one of the most complex and complicated zoning codes in the entire country. It is also fitting that Miami would be where the transect was discovered, and later the first major city in the nation to come clean about its bad zoning diet and adopt a form-based code, named Miami 21.

MIAMI AND THE DISCOVERY OF THE TRANSECT

Andres Duany would later recount in one of his memoirs: *"While idling in Miami Beach, I remarked to Douglas [his brother] that I found its particular urban grid somewhat disorienting. He said, 'Let me show you how to understand it.' We began another linear walk—an urban one this time—from Ocean Drive on the east crossing the city to West Avenue. He said, 'Instead of understanding the urbanism as a collection of monuments or images, randomly visited, learn to walk cities across their grain in both directions a disciplined manner—walk a transect.' This was the first time that I had heard the term."*

Successional development of plants within a natural transect.

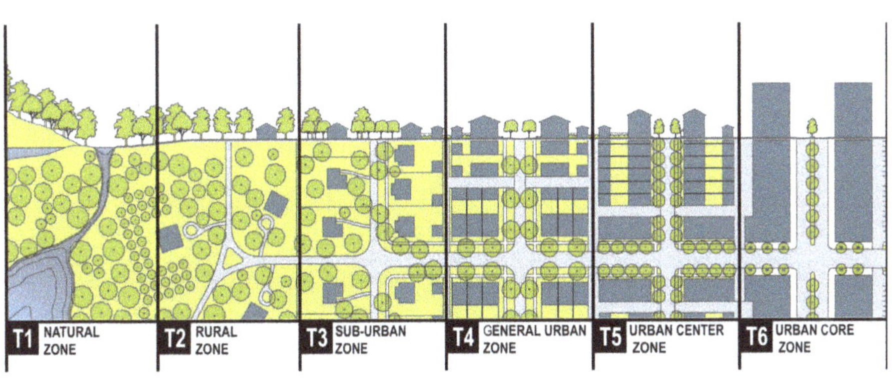

Duany and Plater-Zyberk's urban to rural transect of deveopment.

This way of seeing the metropolis that he now calls home would create an obsession within Duany. He would spend much of his life evangelizing the need to see cities through the lens of the transect. He, along with Elizabeth Plater-Zyberk, were founding members of a movement called the New Urbanism. New Urbanism espouses above all, the notion that there are natural laws that governs human settlement and habitation, and these laws are all bound by the hierarchy of the transect. Miami, the emblem of nature's subjugation, would produce an entire intellectual movement dedicated to making human development more closely resemble the development of natural ecosystems.

MERRICK'S INTELLECTUAL DESCENDENTS

Andres Duany and Elizabeth Plater-Zyberk would intently study Merrick's Coral Gables, and would reside within the municipal boundaries of his planned city for decades. They became entralled with his sub-urban, thickly landscaped city. To them, Coral Gables was a city that had maintained a healthy diet throughout its lifetime. Coral Gables was an example of a city that was delightful to drive through, but had also not fallen into the trap of gobbling endless amounts of land for the sole purpose of traffic throughput.

MIAMI'S EXPORTATION OF DOMESTIC BLISS

Duany and Plater-Zyberk would spend decades translating the designs of highly thoughtful suburbs of Merrick's era into contemporary suburban community designs across the United States. Through the lens of the transect and a fascination with natural processes of succession, Miami's emergent manifesto for suburban domestic bliss was spread across the country.

STUDIO MIAMI

Studio Miami challenges bigness as the ultimate architecture. In 2016, Nicolas Delgado Alcega approached his architectural mentors, Adib Cure and Carie

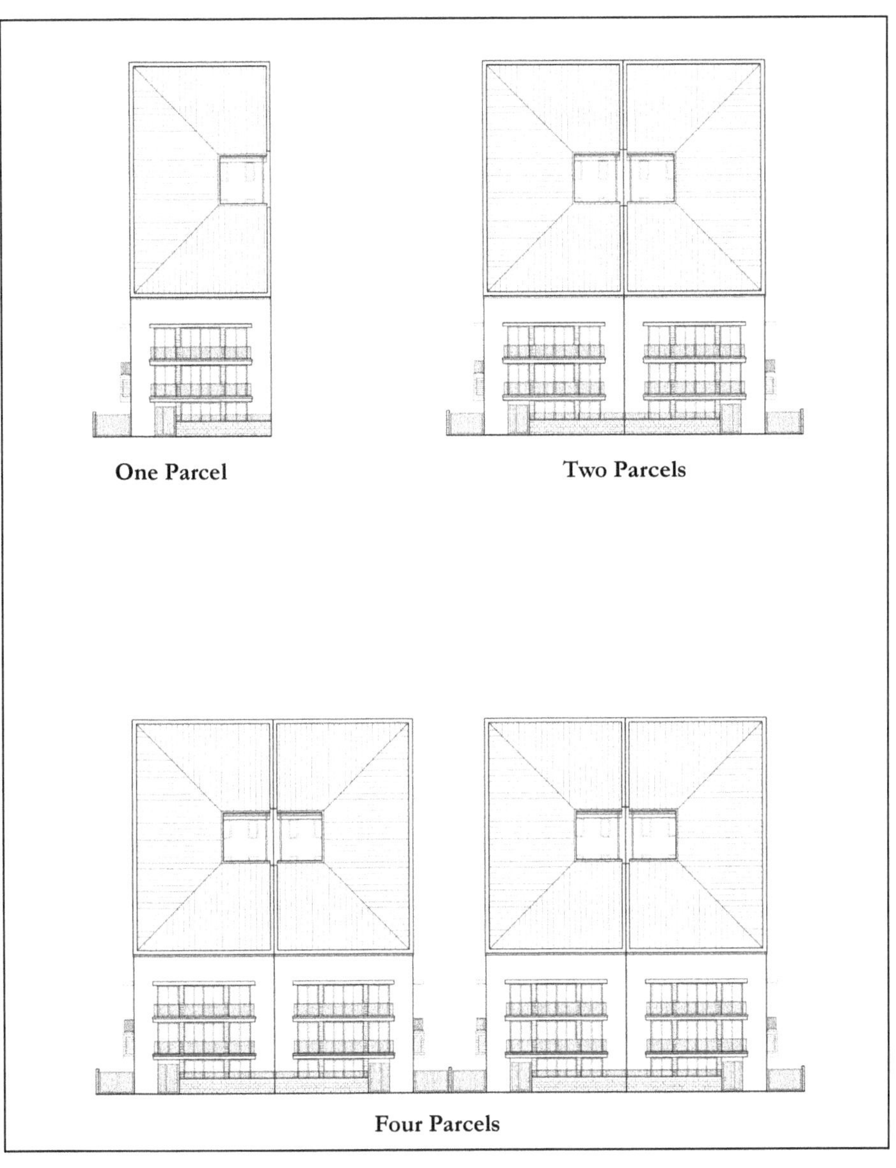

STUDIO MIAMI'S DIAGRAMS FOR CASA FLORIDA.

Penabad, with the proposition of commissioning them to design a project for his family. The two architects encouraged him to take on the project himself, suggesting that he should recruit his friends and colleagues for the project. Studio Miami was born. Four core members would carry out the majority of the studio's work: Nicolas Delgado-Alcega, Claudia Ansorena, Rogelio Cadena, and Gerardo Delgadillo. Spanning a multitude of sites, the group began to develop their design methodology. A simple restoration project turned into an interior design exercise, and then a brand new building design, then another. For young architects, their work spanned an impressive range. From historic preservation to ground-up projects, Studio Miami was a dynamo of a design firm.

This group of Latin American architects' design for one building in particular consciously serves as a manifesto for development of small-scale apartment buildings under Miami's relatively new zoning code, Miami 21. (Developed by Duany and Plater-Zyberk's firm, the 21 in the code's title representing that it was written for a 21st century city.)

Studio Miami's manifesto is titled "CASA FLORIDA: A proposition for the betterment of a city through small scaled development." Studio Miami describes what called the project into action: *"Miami is suburban, and where it is not, its violent soaring into the sky leaves scars in between."* Studio Miami's prescription for this scarring? The healing salve of missing middle scale housing to transition between the city's single family homes and its skyscrapers. Though projects in Miami had been achieving this middle-scaled density for over a decade, what had to change was the development tactics.

"Miami's conventional development tactic: that of redeveloping blocks rather than lots at a time... Within this context, we find our project and purpose... We have looked South and found the courtyard, the binding element that ties Miami to its sister city of Havana and the region at large. Given Miami's geographic location, sub-tropical climate and migration of Caribbean and

Latin American peoples, the courtyard finds itself as a quitessential model to work upon... CASA FLORIDA is more than just a building; it presents the city with a typological variant of the courtyard that [challenges] the relationship of the street, block, building, and unit that we are accustomed [to] in Miami."

This was the stroke of genius that Miami needed. Hearkening back to Sewell's sawn-off piece of Tuttle's Miami Hotel, CASA FLORIDA is incomplete. CASA FLORIDA relies upon community. The community that Miami craves, but is too prideful and headstrong to admit it needs. The architects of Studio Miami had stumbled upon the solution to the question Miami's zoning code begged: How does a city design community and transcendent architecture at the same time?

CASA FLORIDA rose above the gaudy, plastic surgery-like form of the completely isolated architect. It also rose above the backward-looking, kitch interpretations of community that so many New Urbanists remained mired in. CASA FLORIDA stood on its own, but invited the parcel next door to engage. Instead of crossed arms, CASA FLORIDA extended a hand to the not-yet built building next door which shall inevitably block its view of the City skyline.

"CASA FLORIDA is a re-evaluation of the wide held theory that living has to either be in isolation or congestion, in peace or in hostility... As the first small scale, urban project built on a T4 zone in Miami, CASA FLORIDA is an invitation to recognize that we can build humane communities and neighborhoods that we love, and that we can do so with the zeitgeist of our time and place."

The manifesto pamphlet for CASA FLORIDA ends with an image of blocks filled with the project; a project meant to reproduce and flourish through different hands and by different developers.

CASA FLORIDA was more resilient because of its smallness. CASA FLORIDA was developed at the scale of the lot. This, more than all others, is the project that stands ready to take over the city, not through a single architectural act, but through reproduction.

Wynwood yard in 2014.

Wynwood Yard in 2017.

THE CONSERVATIONIST PIONEER

Rewind two years from the inception of Studio Miami. Della Heiman, a Cincinnati native, had a growing interest in both cooking and food culture. She studied food sustainability and was greatly interested in solving the problems of "food deserts", which are developed areas without easily accessible fresh food. In 2014, after graduating from school, she arrived in Miami, deciding it was the time to open up a restaurant. After spending months combing through dozens of properties, she realized that the conventional route of renting a brick and mortar space would not work for her. Rents were high, and the terms provided by the landlords were too rigid.

The most successful areas of Miami were too hostile for Heiman, and she realized there must be others like her who were seeking somewhere less developed with a younger ecology. The environments of Downtown, Miami Beach, or Brickell were already highly developed and had undergone successive processes long ago which served as a barrier to the entry of the pioneer species of primary succession. Eventually, she found a plot of land in Wynwood. The two notable aspects of the lot were a grey food truck and a few coconut palms, which were as alien to the original landscape as the truck. At this time, rents in Wynwood had already risen, but compared to the other sites in Miami, this was a bargain. Heiman bought the food truck off of the man who owned it and signed a lease with the owner of the property. In contrast to the stringent and lengthy contracts Heiman had faced in the more developed areas, the contract she signed was just 3 pages, size 15 font. Heiman had an intuition that renting the somewhat dumpy site was exactly right for the time and place. She used the small amount of capital she had to purchase the truck and lease the land. If Miami had a lack of spaces available to creative entrepreneurs like herself, Heiman could create a place for them. By doing so, she helped balance the financial ecology of the area. Heiman inherited a site with illegal electrical wiring and no plumbing hookup. From the beginning, she set out to do as much as she could with what she had. Making minimal investments in proper plumbing and electrical systems, she went through the zoning approvals process under the City of Miami. The site was not allowed to operate with a liquor license, but Heiman wanted a bar in the middle of the project. Creatively, she was able to find a third party catering company to operate a bar with their catering license. Very few of the patrons who ordered a drink at Wynwood Yard realized the sheer number of legal hoops and processes that had to be jumped through just to serve them. The site became a thriving watering hole for locals and visitors. At night, anyone and everyone came to Wynwood Yard; some dressed in heels, stopping by to grab a bite before taking a ride to South Beach for a night of partying, others in t-shirts and jeans.

Despite the legal creativity employed in the process of establishing Wynwood Yard and creating a social space for the area, it was not a path free of obstacles once the approvals were made. One night after leaving Wynwood Yard to go home and sleep, Heiman was woken up by a phone call from one of her managers, who told her that she had better come back to the bar, as a squad of police offices and a dozen regulatory agencies had arrived to shut down Wynwood Yard. Despite her attempts to find a space that was outside of the restrictive confines of the downtown, Heiman still had to confront the bureaucratic environment. She quickly grabbed every file and physical scrap of evidence that showed she was in compliance and made her way to the Yard to confront the regulators. They told her once she arrived that they were there to arrest her. After hours of carefully pouring over the evidence that Heiman provided, the regulators told her that her establishment was, in fact, legal. Hours after pulling up with the intent of arresting Heiman, the officers told her that she was not under arrest, and that she and her employees could go home. Intimidation tactics and arriving in the dead of night proved unsuccessful, but this didn't prevent the officials from taking a final shot at her. She would later recall: *"They put together a whole report on the Wynwood Yard. They took all of these pictures, they slapped it down on the zoning administrator's desk the next day and basically said to him that I was on drugs. That I was on drugs because I was so calm during our conversation that I must have been high. It wasn't that I was high, I just wasn't afraid of them. Because they're used to walking in bars and people just crying, hysterical. I wasn't afraid of them because I hadn't done anything wrong. I had spent months getting this thing permitted the right way."*

Despite the obstacles, just two and a half years after Heiman, a Midwest native, moved to Miami, the Wynwood Yard had become the source of livelihoods for 130 people, not counting the dozens of individuals who held events and concerts there every month. It has grown from a handful of food trucks into 16 different fully operational companies. Heiman contributed to the advancement of ecological succession within Wynwood. Having advanced the ecology of the neighborhood, the Wynwood Yard was in part a victim of its own success. The neighborhood had become another area so popular that the red-hot market pushed out businesses and residents who couldn't afford the rapidly rising rents.

"There's like 20 new venues that just opened in the past 2 months. Every weekend something new opens, and now its big companies that are coming in here with crazy marketing budgets, crazy programmatic budgets, and we just can't compete with that. We're a local, grassroots organization. We pay every artist that performs on our stage here, and its expensive. Because Wynwood is becoming so saturated and because its attracting so many big players that are just capitalized very differently than we are, I just don't know if we'd be able to survive here forever."[8] Heiman's lease ended in 2019, and Wynwood Yard ceased operations, pushed out by the speculative forces that fed from it's own success.

INTERAMA: THE TRUEST MIAMI HAS (N)EVER BEEN

"Miami with the luxuries of villas, green spaces, trees budding, flowers blooming, avenues and automobiles. Enough to make one utterly sick from so much artifice."

-Le Corbusier [1]

ARTIFICE

Miami has always been a city that self-invents. The development Miami saw during the early and mid-20th century was the most self-invented and artificial of all. The metropolis, drained and cleared of swampy waters, saw a rapidly expanding footprint of tracts of single family homes; filling the land between its multiple developed nodes and westwards deeper into the Everglades.[2] Following the general suburban trends that defined post-war America, the neighborhoods that had specific identities started to drown within a monoculturous urban fabric that seemed to ooze up from the ground into every undeveloped crevice. The proliferation of the mechanical pump and advances in canal engineering meant the ecological barriers to settling the land were removed. Once the swampland has been wrung dry like a sponge, it yields complete ecological control. A lack of silt means structurally intense development can occur pretty much anywhere. Inversely, a high water table means that, if you want a lake, all you have to do is dig one up and receive instant gratification as water invariably fills the depression to the brim. If you want to part the waters and build out into the bay, simply dump a bit of soil where needed, and presto, instant land. This somewhat low bar for

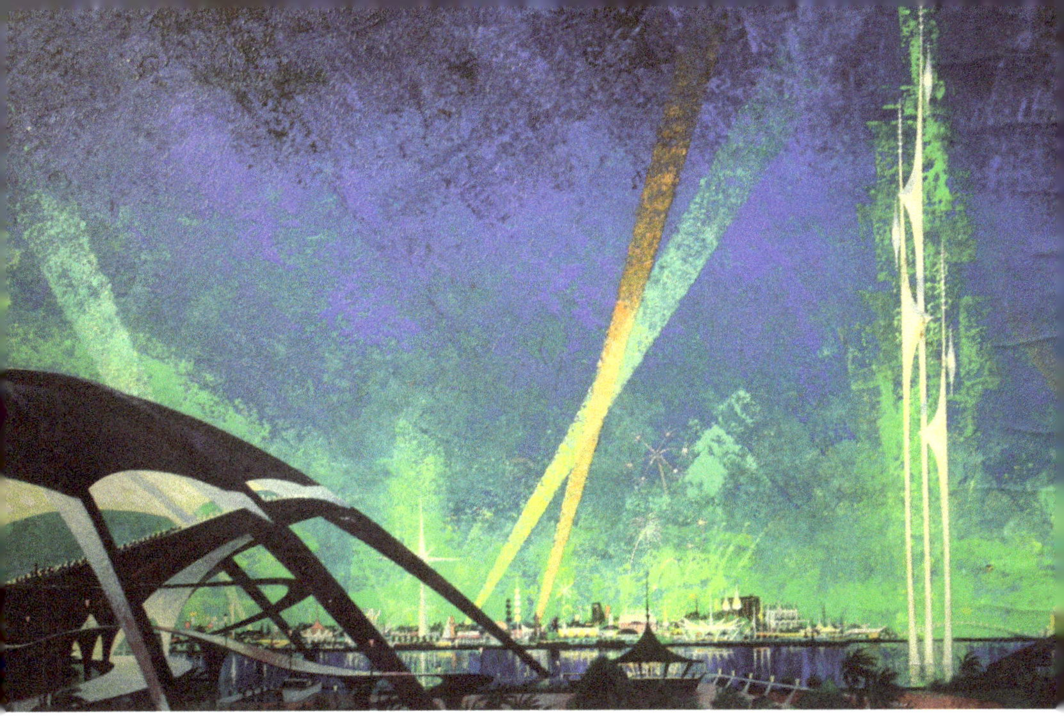

A night view of the Interama site design.

Aerial view looking South, the freshly dredged and outlined land For Interama in Biscayne Bay.

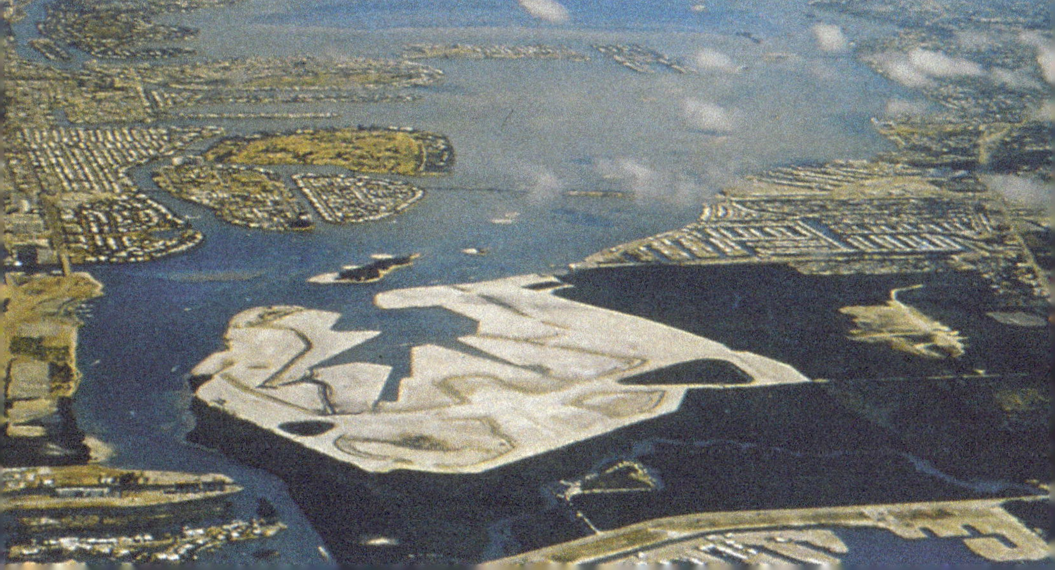

ecological mastery enabled extremely low quality and monotonous development throughout the entire region. Artifice, however, is part of the intelligent architect's toolkit, and many notable projects in Miami have made smart use of the artificial. Enter Interama, a daring project for an entire new city; a model for an idealized "international neighborliness" that prefigured Epcot. Culminating in a design that would, unconsciously, compel the city for a century, the story of Interama created the five aspirations that Miami is still unconsciously acting upon today.

GENESIS

As long as it has been a part of the United States, Miami has been a node connecting the U.S. with Central and South America. For the majority of the city's history, proposals have been made to formalize this connection in a single project. Attempts were even made by the Sewell Brothers as early as the 1920s.[3] In 1949, an over two-decade long search for the project that would express Miami's five aspirations began. It was a project that would involve 6 presidents, 34 nations, and many designers whose culminated efforts would yield a design that prophesized Miami's future without ever being realized.

The Sewells' ideas for an inter-American project fell to the side during late 1920s when the land boom ended, but their successors saw increasing utility for the idea after business ties and air travel between Miami and Cuba increased dramatically. A real effort, however, was not established until 1949, when a committee was established to propose a cultural and economic exchange center in Miami. After securing a resolution for federal funding in 1950, the Florida legislature created the Inter-American Center Authority (IACA) to plan out the Inter-American Center, also called INTERAMA.

The timing of the project was no coincidence, and planning efforts could not have started at a better time. Miami saw business activity explode sky-high as its economic ties with the rest of the Americas strengthened. It became clear that there might be a desire among Miami's international hemispheric interests

DRAWING FROM MIAMI NEWS COLLECTION, 1963, ARTIST UNKNOWN.

to house within the city an Inter-American Center. Interama was conceived as a permanent international exposition of the Americas. Functionally, it would combine cultural, educational, and trade activities, in a form echoing the World's Fairs of Chicago and New York. The designs for Interama yielded exceedingly thought-provoking schemes for a "tropical civic urbanism" in Miami.[4] This was Super-Tropicalism realized. A 1,600-acre bayfront site was selected, five miles north of downtown Miami. The geography of the site was perfect for a utopian project that would function on the scale of a small city. The shallow waters of Biscayne Bay made dredging and filling to create land uncomplicated. The tropical weather lent itself to outdoor activity year-round, making comfortable public space easily achievable.

CONCEPTION

In 1950, a group of five local architects was assembled. Robert Fitch Smith led the design team including Russel T. Pancoast, Alfred Browning Parker, John E. Peterson, and Robert Law Weed. The members of the team would go down in history for their individual contributions to the region's architecture and their lasting impact on Miami's aesthetic. They designed buildings that used shade, ventilation, and screening that responded to the climate. Their designs interpreted the history of Miami, including the Florida Cracker and Art Deco styles before they were popularly known as such. They designed buildings that were of their time, but spoke to Miami's history. What this team designed for Interama was not a statement, what they designed was invisible. They held a mirror up to Miami through which the city could, for the first time, see itself.

The local architects were relentlessly obsessed with the tropical and the aquatic. Renderings showed people walking from concrete canopies to planted oases, both of which were spaced appropriately to fend off the direct sunlight without losing appreciation for it. They drew concrete as a plastic, interpretive medium without directly mimicking natural elements. Rather, their forms complemented

ALL THREE
RENDERINGS FROM
THE INTERAMA
COLLECTION AT
HISTORYMIAMI
MUSEUM ARCHIVES

the landscape and, in certain moments, enshrined nature. For example, in the image on the middle of the adjacent page, a palm is shown growing up and through a circular hole in a cantilevered plane of concrete. The purpose of the concrete, as drawn, is for nothing other than to highlight the palm's slender form. Sensuous architectural metaphors like this are seen throughout rendered vignettes of the project.

As Jules Verne would predict a hundred years in advance, Florida would become the launchpad for humankind's first expedition to the moon. The early drawings to come from this group of architects would also echo this prediction in their fascination with the space age. An observatory was depicted (bottom of previous page,) open to the night sky, with visitors shown using the giant pieces of equipment. The observatory sat under a domed pavilion that was shown in the middle of a lake, in an odd fusion that was becoming of Miami - the nautical and the cosmic. The dome was drawn surrounded by a supporting cast of palm trees, whose silhouettes created an organic outline that complemented the perfect form and shiny exterior of the dome, which rose from the water like an air

The group of local architects posing over a set of drawings. Standing from left are; Robert Law Weed, Russell T. Pancoast, Alfred B. Parker and John E. Peterson. Robert Fitch Smith is seated.

Hugh Ferris, master renderer. Ferris elevated the work of the local architects from thoughtful, contextual modernism to the Super-Tropical.

Image on facing page: An early Hugh Ferris rendering, before his fusion of Sphere and Tower .

bubble. The bubble featured, under its concrete overhang, murals of galaxies and planets. An exhibit dedicated to humankind's conquering of space was situated in a lake dredged to symbolize the conquering of the earth.

SPHERE AND TOWER, MARRIED

Miami is a city well acquainted with smuggling operations. The importation of the same spirit which birthed Manhattanism was not simply brought to Miami in a single go. The covert importation of what would become Super-Tropicalism was a decades-long process that began but did not end with Flagler. Hugh Ferriss was commissioned to join the team of local architects, bringing with him the visualization techniques that made famous the supernatural elements of New York. Having visualized New York's World Fair of 1939, Ferriss had in his mind the two most powerful geometric constructions of any architectural expo: Wallace K. Harrison's designs for the tower and the sphere. After working through the schemes, however, Ferriss realized that there was a new emergent geometry. This geometry would embody the spirit not only of Interama, but of Miami itself. Ferriss conceived a marriage of the two forms, sphere and tower,

THIS SKETCH FROM FERRIS' WORK ON **INTERAMA** SHOWS HIS PROCESS OF MARRYING THE TWO FORMS, SPHERE AND TOWER, INTO THE ARCHWAY.

Sphere and tower arrive in Miami.

Ferris' rendering for Interama, with archways realized.

into a single geometry- the geometry of the arch. Ferriss drew three concrete arches: each would represent part of the Americas- North, Central, and South. The entire hemisphere was to be represented in this central gesture, poured from concrete which would inevitably use local oolitic limestone as aggregate. With this form, Ferriss had achieved the supernatural: ultimate identity within a single geometric form. Miami was to be the Archway, the entrance between the United States and the rest of the Americas.

Just as he had in Manhattan, Ferriss unearthed a subterranean collective dialogue that was occuring under the murky cultural surface of the metropolis. The typologies of the city in the mid-20th century were in an emergent state, impossible to identify without retrospective clarity. Up until this point, Miami's metropolitan region was haunted by the same equation that had struck the rest of the developed world. Until this time, all of Miami's major planned projects imported non-native architecture and, using fake or non-local materials, attempted to narrate Miami's reality through the fiction of other locales. Coral Gables had its myriad of villages with Dutch South African, Chinese, French, and Italian architectural themes; Opa Locka with its Moorish theme, and likewise Vizcaya with its Mediterranean Revival theme. All succumbed to the formula Rem Koolhaas surmised would "haunt architecture forevermore..."

technology + cardboard (or any other flimsy material) = reality

Interama held within it the unheralded solution to this equation. In designing this exposition, the architects stumbled upon an master-planned scheme, yielding buildings that, according to Ferriss, "differ completely from the "Spanish-American style" popular in the '20s."[5] Miami's answer that would restore narrative and purpose to the practice of architecture...

transcendence of nature + integration of nature = the supernatural

Indeed, the supernatural can be discovered in any locale given a proper amount of time. In New York, Manhattanism emerged as the result of the ecological restriction of the peninsula and the anthropic invention of the grid. In Miami, Super-Tropicalism emerged from the pliable ecology of the land and the cultural integration of the non-native. Ferris manifested Manhattanism, his representations describing humankind's struggle in the 20th century. Man, constrained by nature, fights to create order in a hostile world.

Ferris prophesized Super-Tropicalism, and humankind's struggle of the 21st century. Man, having beaten nature into submission, must find purpose beyond survival. Miami leads the world in this struggle, where purpose requires a balance of hedonism and stewardship.

FERRISS, FOILED

The project seemed to have every green light. In 1952, President Truman signed legislation calling upon officials and agencies of the federal government to work with the IACA. He also invited all nations of the Americas to participate in the project. The City of Miami conferred upon the Authority 1700 acres it had acquired previously for an airport.[6] In 1955, the IACA negotiated with Lehman Brothers of New York, producing a plan authorizing them to issue $70 million in bonds to back the project. A report was produced claiming the park would be "debt-free, self-sustaining, and profitable within six years of operation" with 17.5 million visitors per year projected. Investors were quite confident and Lehman Brothers' Frank Morse recommended that the name INTERAMA be copyrighted. They were following in the steps of Walt Disney who was receiving significant income from the rights to the name "Disneyland", the project in Anaheim, California that had opened in 1955.[7] In March of 1956, with two weeks before the closing date for the money lent by the Lehman Brothers, board members spoke publicly about a 1958 opening for Interama. The future for the project seemed rosy, but the project would soon be struck by fate. Incidentally, Bobby Lehman of Lehman Brothers had flown from Miami to Washington sitting next to the president of Pan-American Airlines. As they flew to Washington, Lehman described the project and asked for a second opinion. Lehman was then peppered with reasons why the park couldn't succeed. Revenue, attendance, and engagement projections were called into question during this conversation. Disneyland in Anaheim had just opened with major cost overruns; originally budgeted for $9 million, Disneyland cost $17 million by the end of construction. Disney's finances were stretched thin. Many thought the project would leave him in financial ruin. Interama's construction was projected to cost over four times that amount and was planned to be 10 times the size.[8] Exacerbating the bad timing of Bobby Lehman's airplane conversation, the bond market had suddenly entered its worst period in two decades. The Lehman Brothers saw this dangerous killer of real estate projects on the horizon: rising interest rates. As lenders saw higher yields in government bonds, their appetite for more risky investments such as Interama fell. Without the magical powers of leveraged loans behind them, private investors would have a difficult time getting the project financed. Lehman, having returned to the cold, sharp air of New York from the intoxicating tropical heat of Miami, felt as though he had just sobered up. He pulled out of the deal.

THE MOST MAGICAL PLACE ON EARTH

Disneyland achieved 3.6 million visitors its first year. The board of the IACA sought collaboration with Walt Disney, as its prospects began to dwindle. Desperate for an investor, the IACA did its best to present the idea as a win to Disney. After hearing the entire scheme for the International park, with an estimated 17.5 million visitors per year, Disney was impressed, but the outcome of this impression was not what the committee foresaw. Having learned his lesson in Anaheim, Disney didn't want to deal with the troubles of civic discourse and governance interfering with his creative control. Just a few years after hearing the pitch for Interama, on the 22nd of November 1963, Disney boarded a plane to look at an isolated area of swampy land to the south of Orlando. *"That's it,"* he decreed, as the pointed down towards the future site of Disney World. In 1965, Disney announced plans for his own new project that would create a new kind of America, not just a theme park. There would be rides, of course, but *"by far the most important part of our Florida project,"* he pledged, *"will be our Experimental Prototype Community of Tomorrow. We'll call it Epcot."*[9] Why try to work within the confines of democracy, when you can build a development in the wilderness and privatize everything? The monopolization of Main Street, U.S.A. had begun. The committee's predictions of 17.5 million visitors per year, pitched so eagerly to Disney, did not count on a competing project. When Disney World opened in 1971, it saw 20.49 million visitors in its first year.

FINAL MODEL ASSEMBLING THE WORK OF THE SEVEN ARCHITECTS: PAUL RUDOLPH, EDWARD DURRELL STONE, JOSE LUIS SERT, LOUIS KAHN, HARRY WEESE, MARCEL BREUER, AND MINORU YAMASAKI.

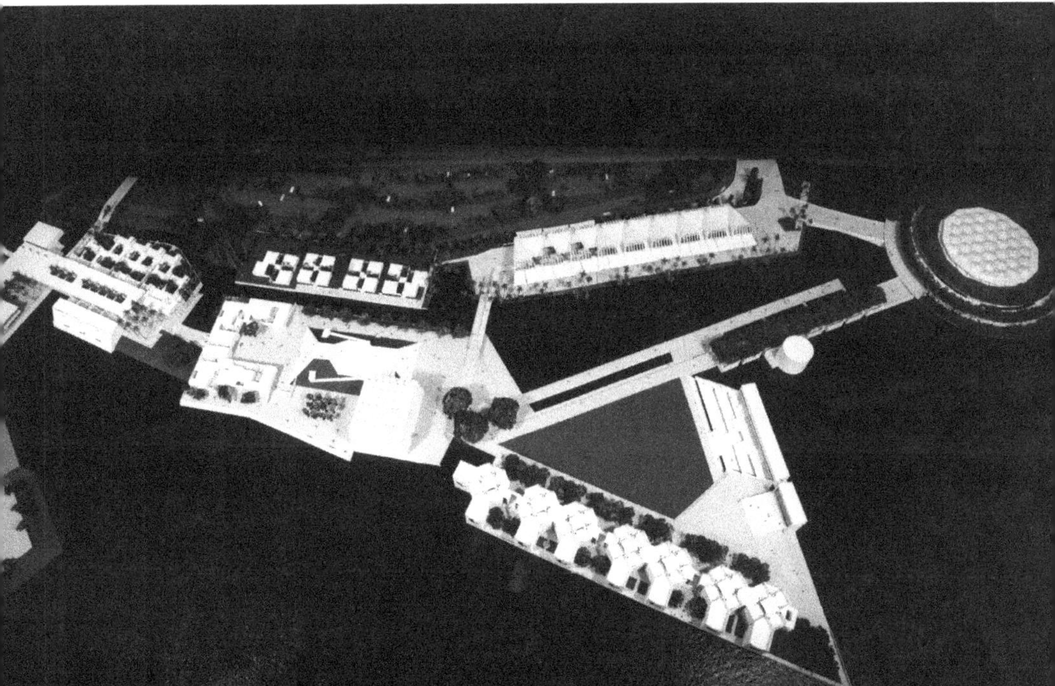

PAUL RUDOLPH - INTERNATIONAL BAZAAR

RUDOLPH STATED THAT INTERAMA AVOIDED THE "TYPICAL UNBEARABLE INCOHERENCE" OF CONTEMPORARY AMERICAN CITY PLANNING. HE WENT ON TO SAY THAT "(INTERAMA'S) BUILDINGS ARE DEPENDENT ON WATER, WALKWAYS, AND PLANTING. THEY SHOULD NOT BE THOUGHT OF AS INDIVIDUAL STRUCTURES, BUT RATHER AS A WHOLE."[10] RUDOLPH WAS NATIONALLY FAMOUS FOR HIS DESIGNS UTILIZING CONCRETE, AND AT THIS TIME HAD ALREADY ESTABLISHED THE "SARASOTA SCHOOL OF DESIGN" IN SOUTH FLORIDA.

Edward Durrell Stone - United States

Stone, known for his design of the Museum of Modern Art, as well as his Art-Deco masterpiece of Radio City Music Hall, was another designer hailing from Manhattan who was complicit in the smuggling of the Supernatural into Miami. Having also designed the U.S. Pavillion for the World's Fair in Brussels and the U.S. Embassy in New Dehli, Stone was well fit for his design task: Interama's U.S. Pavillion.

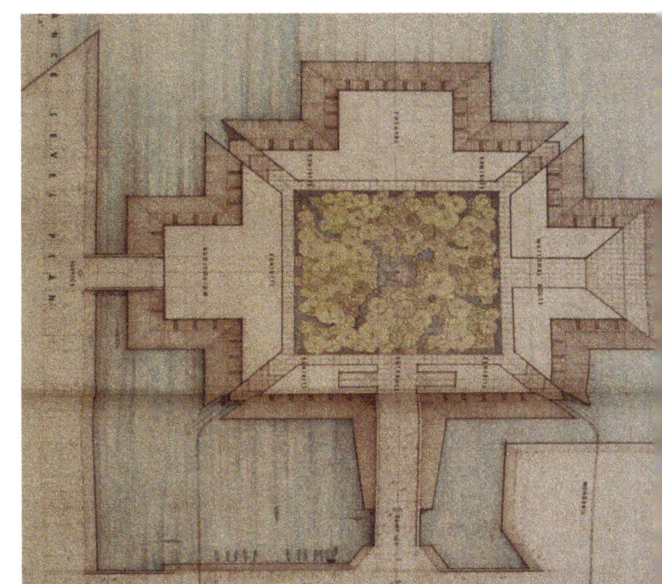

Jose Luis Sert - Western South America - Bolivia, Chile, Colombia, Ecuador, Peru, and Venezuela

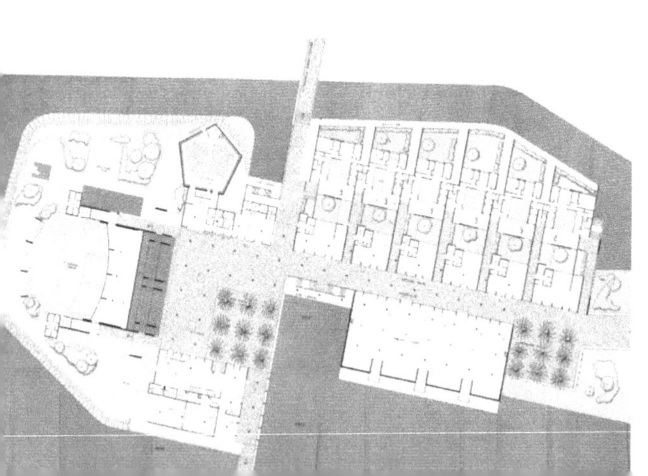

Sert was a champion of downtowns and "the heart of the city" within modernist planning practices. Speaking about the project, he said "Interama has the same principles and size as the center of a city. There is a distillation of the designs and open spaces so they all fit together... sequels, spaces, and a variety of buildings that serve as the true-scaled experiment in what is today called urban design."

Kahn, who famously said that "The street is a room by agreement," designed a triangular section of the campus that faced a triangular plaza. Kahn was likely unaware of the historical significance of his prescription for a palm-lined promenade that enclosed the plaza. His prescription was foreshadowed by the decree of Flagler in 1897 for a palm grove at his Royal Palm Hotel.

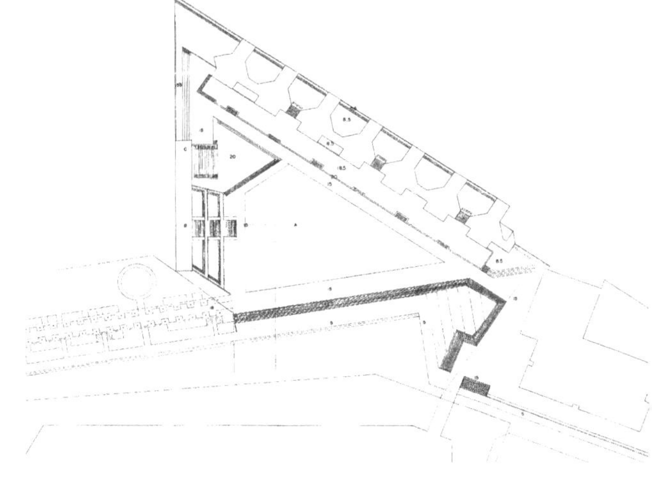

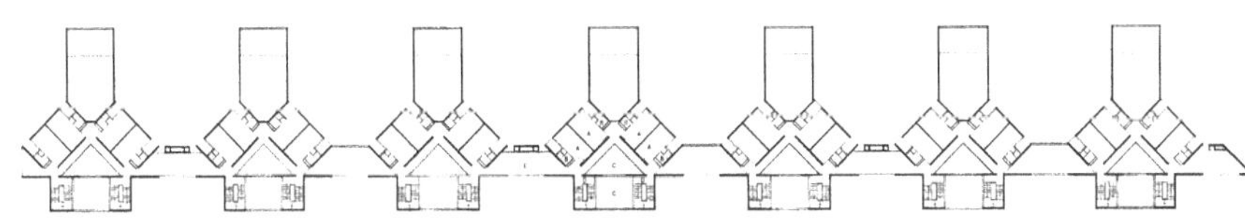

HARRY WEESE - CARIBBEAN NATIONS - CUBA, THE DOMINICAN REPUBLIC, HAITI, JAMAICA, AND TRINIDAD-TOBAGO

WEESE WAS AN EXPERT IN TIMBER, BRICK, AND MOST RELEVANT TO THE MIAMI LOCALE, CONCRETE. HE WAS EXTREMELY PROLIFIC, HIS FIRM PRODUCING MORE THAN 200 NEW BUILDINGS AND MAJOR RENOVATIONS. LIKE HIS PEERS SELECTED TO PARTICIPATE IN INTERAMA, HE HAD EXPERIENCE IN PUBLIC WORKS, HAVING DESIGNED A U.S. EMBASSY IN GHANA. THE LONG, LINEAR BUILDING HE DESIGNED WAS FLANKED ON ONE SIDE WITH STEPS LEADING TO THE WATER, AND PALM TREES ON THE OTHER.

MARCEL BREUER - EASTERN LATIN AMERICA - ARGENTINA, BRAZIL, PARAGUAY, AND URUGUAY

BREUER LEFT EUROPE IN THE 1930S TO TEACH AT HARVARD AND PRACTICE ARCHITECTURE IN AMERICA. HE WAS ONE OF THE LEADING FORCES IN THE SPREAD OF MODERNISM GLOBALLY. PROTÈGÈ TO WALTER GROPIUS AT THE BAUHAUS, BREUER WOULD SPAWN MORE SIGNATURE ARCHITECTS OF THE 20TH CENTURY, INCLUDING PHILIP JOHNSON, PAUL RUDOLPH, AND I.M. PEI, DURING HIS PROFESSORSHIP AT HARVARD. THE LOCATION OF HIS DESIGN FOR EASTERN LATIN AMERICA'S SECTION WAS CENTRAL TO THE OVERALL PLAN.

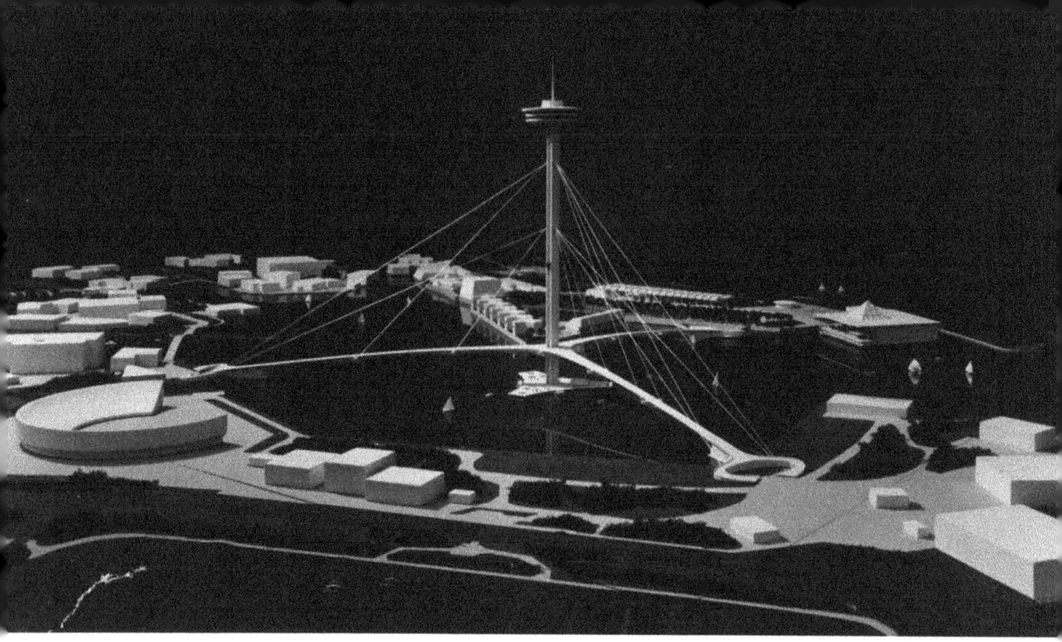

Minoru Yamasaki - Central Tower

(Image Above) Regression to the tower as the unifying element - Yamasaki was brought on after the fact in the late 1960s, in an attempt to create a focal point which would unify the new proposal. At first glance, the tower would appear to be a rip-off of the design for the Space Needle in Seattle. Though the Space Needle's design was published before Yamasaki's design, Ferris' drawing for a tower (left side of image below) preceded the Space Needle's design by at least 3 years.

(Image Below) Hugh Ferriss - Rendering Published in The Florida Architect, February 1956. The first sketch for the Space Needle appeared publicly in 1959.

THE CREATION OF EDEN

In 1966, a year after Disney World was announced, six all-star architects were assembled for a second round of design, in an attempt to resurrect the project. This team represented a portfolio of extreme international acclaim, consisting of Paul Rudolph, Edward Durrell Stone, Jose Luis Sert, Louis Kahn, Harry Weese, and Marcel Breuer. They would build upon the Super-Tropical scheme of the local architects, adding to it the five aspirations for what Miami would realize in the next century. With complete technological mastery over the landscape, the architects had the ability to prescribe not only where buildings sit on the land, but also the existence of the land itself. Able to control the indoor climate, the architects could designate zones of climate utilizing methods of refrigeration, ventilation, and shade. With the complete palette of the tropics at their fingertips, the architects could prescribe exactly where nature would be constructed. Unknowingly obeying Flagler's decree that coconut palms were to be planted everywhere, and symbolizing the omnipresence of the integrated non-native, the new group of six architects included these trees in almost every perspective rendering they drew. Integrating the geology of the region, most of the buildings were once again designed to be built of reinforced concrete. The project was fantastic, both in scale and spirit.

THE DOWNFALL OF MIAMI'S GREATEST PROJECT

Minoru Yamasaki was brought in late to this iteration of Interama's design, and his intervention would represent the beginning of the end for the project; Hugh Ferris' discovery of Miami's perfect form, the arch, was forgotten and replaced instead by a mediocre copy of Ferriss' design for a tower within Interama. It is still unknown if the design for Seattle's Space Needle had borrowed from Ferriss' drawings for Interama, which were published three years before the initial program for the Space Needle was conceived.

CRUMBLE

The success of the project relied on Latin American governmental involvement. In 1967, 17 Latin American heads of state committed, in writing, to be represented in the project for Interama. 11 sent their own planners to begin selecting parcels upon which to build their pavilions.

However, despite the initial enthusiasm, no real support would come from Latin America. This period from the late 60s to the 80s would be marked by military coups and governmental instability. Sentiment in Latin American countries also soured after repeated U.S. interventions in governmental affairs. Desperate for private funding, the IACA began rapidly proposing new ideas for the site, making the project seem more and more like a scam to the public with each desperate utterance. Michael Hoover wrote on Interama's spiral: "Thus, a stadium for the newly-established Miami Dolphins professional football team was on the agenda for a time, only to be replaced by thoughts of an automobile racing track, the track quickly giving way to a marina with berths for 300 yachts, a 200 room luxury hotel, retail shops, a seaplane ramp, customs and immigration facilities, a water transportation fleet, and marine repair service... a high speed roller coaster, a zoo, a symphony and opera hall, ballet and music theater, dramatic arts theater with experimental repertory company, art gallery, and museum."

The flexibility of the geography allowed for anything and everything to be built, and in the end, Interama could not raise money to do anything but invent land for the next developers of the site. Upon the silt dredged up for Interama now sits a public park, Oleta River State Park, and a college campus, the FIU Biscayne Bay Campus. The project would not be realized, however the spirit of Interama became manifest in the Five Aspirations of Miami.

Drawings of Hugh Ferriss' design for the three arches.

THE FIVE ASPIRATIONS
OF MIAMI

PHOTOGRAPH BY QIAZI CHEN

Wealth (Condominiums)

THE LIES WE TELL UNTIL THEY COME TRUE

In Miami real estate, salesmanship has always preceded reality; whether it was selling water in the hopes that it may one day become land, or land in the hopes it may one day become waterfront property. The architectural expression of this delirious, invented reality was invoked in the 1970s by the young and avant-garde founders of the Miami firm Arquitectonica. The late 70s saw the proliferation of many skylines in the South, but in Miami, something special was happening. The desire for differentiation, in real estate speak, "a unique product," had gripped developers around the city. Considerations of cost and efficiency had never been the driver of Miami's great projects, and this time was no different. Developers were willing to go to great lengths in order to catch the potential condo buyer's eye, and architects who could help achieve this goal were highly sought after. Contrivance was popular, gaudy was in vogue, and opulence was all the rage.

MONUMENT IN THE SKY

In 1981, Miami was mired in violence and corruption. That year, the entire Miami Police Academy's rookie class later either went to jail or died a violent death.[1] The crime rate was the highest in the nation. Further stressing the City, Miami had an immigrant crisis; thousands of homeless Cubans were living in tents under the downtown expressway. Despite the lack of refugee housing, the luxury housing market was red hot. Arquitectonica was commissioned to design the Atlantis, which finished construction in 1982. The blockbuster hit

of the firm took the city by storm. It was the perfect expression of everything that was boisterous, idiosyncratic, loud, and yet somehow dignified; it was the perfect expression of Miami. As T.D. Allman observed, most people called it *"the condo with the big hole cut out of the middle."*[2] But the Atlantis was not a condo building with a hole punched out of it, it was a preserved piece of the sky surrounded by condos. The Atlantis was conceptually defined by its centrally placed orifice. The rhythm of the windows was broken on the building's side by this square cutout which housed a jacuzzi, a red spiral staircase, and a lone coconut palm in the center. The palm was the perfect monument for Miami, where the non-native conquers all. Miami, where the coconut palm can go from landing for the first time by boat to being enshrined on the throne of the city within two generations. The Atlantis was, and still is, the greatest monument to immigrants in Miami, and by extension, it is a monument to every citizen of the city.

The opulence of a luxury high rise, juxtaposed with thousands of homeless refugees just miles away, rejected any urbanism of good intentions that pervaded other cities at the time. The narcissism and heroism of Miami's citizens was enshrined in the Atlantis. Unlike the lifeless multiplication of the land that characterizes many condominium towers built before and afterwards, the Atlantis preserves the monument of the palm tree suspended in the sky and guarded on all sides by the best armor a monument can have: private real estate owned by the wealthy.

MULTIPLICATION OF THE LAND

Most towers in Miami are not noteworthy for their design. Many tower parks are plots of land where the same building design is stamped upon the landscape multiple times in a row, resulting in a machine-like monotony. This monotony begins to produce a strange effect; these white-painted clusters begin to seem as if they are moving, traveling as part of a herd. Their silent

Facing Page- The Atlantis Condominium Building. Photograph by Qiazi Chen.

frozen procession is mirrored in the very real procession of cruise ships that depart from Miami's Biscayne Bay every day. It is as if the buildings themselves want to return to the water.

LONG LIVE THE DICTATOR

There is a saying in the world of Miami real estate: "long live the dictator." These four words imply, truthfully, that much of what drives Miami's real estate market is its perception as a safe haven to park international wealth from all over the globe. When political instability arises in a country, undoubtedly some members of the bourgeois class will find the need to stash their riches where they are safe from government seizure. Foreign investment has fueled red-hot speculation time and time again, playing into the boom-bust dynamic of Miami real estate.

HYPER-AMENITIZATION

Condominiums see stiff competition from other housing real estate "products" in Miami. Miami is the city of the single-family home, the city of the lushly landscaped garden and private pool. Miami is the city of driving to work while being blasted by vapor-cooled air at 8 in the morning when it's already 80 degrees outside. To compete with this, condominium buildings must create new amenities. From olympic-sized swimming pools an elevator ride away, to spas complete with "biohacking" rooms, to car elevators that allow you to have a private garage inside your 60th story unit. A city where private, personal luxuries are held in the highest regard, Miami is constantly one-upping its most ostentatious of amenities. All of these amenities can be traced to the Atlantis, the city's most fantastic signature building that unintentionally monumentalized Miami's immigrants.

View of cruise ships
along Dodge Island.

Multiplied condominiums.
hotograph by Qiazi Chen.

Multiplied Condominiums

PALACE
(SINGLE FAMILY HOUSE)

"Miami is a city of houses, a "domestic city." In this truly modern city, desperately lacking public architecture, the domestic realm and the landscape predominate in the collective eye. Houses and trees are Miami's true monuments, and even its rare public attractions - its grand hotels, the Deering Estate, the Deco District, etc. - partake of the domestic."
Jean-François Lejeune, *Architecture of the Tropics*

DOMUS TROPICUS

Miami: located at the very tip of America's Floridian peninsula that thrusts itself into a completely different climate zone. Florida was known to many Americans in the mid-20th century as the only part of the continental United States that could be considered "tropical". As millions of Americans had experienced Miami temporarily on vacation, some decided that they wanted to relocate to the tropical environment. These newcomers had to collectively learn how to live in Miami. Igor B. Polevitzky would address Florida's other architects, stating that *"Floridians as a whole are a little different from the average American for pretty obvious reasons. We have moved here, and in the moving we did more than just move to another house or another state - we have moved into a totally new pioneering environment and climate. We have moved spiritually, as well as physically."*
Miami would become a city of the detached home in the garden, populated in large part by Americans from the northern states who had no experience living in their new climate.

VILLA VIZCAYA: THE IDEAL KITSCH

On Christmas Day of 1916, James Deering lands at Villa Vizcaya on his yacht *Nepenthe.* The Villa took 4 years to construct, and this is the day he officially begins its occupancy. A Christmas present to himself, he wakes up the next morning in his personal suite on the second floor and makes his way into the bathroom. He leans over an ingeniously designed sink piped for hot water, directly in front of the French doors which face outward from the bathroom towards Biscayne Bay. He turns the faucet, bringing heated water to the stand, knowing that his personal bathroom was designed to be at the center of the facade, in the nucleus of the design. Millions of dollars spent and hundreds of laborers' efforts have built up to this moment. Technology and architecture have come together in this enormous estate to culminate in a single experience. The villa's owner has an incredible view while he shaves his face in the morning.

ASPIRATIONAL SPRAWL

So many of Miami's monuments being of domestic character, the American trope of "keeping up with the Joneses" is exponentiated in Miami. Upon driving by one of the many ostentatious villas within the city, the mind begins to conjure aspirations. A plot of land, all one's own. A large house, built within a privately owned slice of fabricated nature. The single-family home, in all its glorious opulence and infrastructural inefficiency, became everyone's goal. Thus, in the same wave of aspirational sprawl as the rest of the nation, Miami's low-density housing spread. Enabled by the automobile, homebuyers drove all over the newly drained swampland; the farther from one of Miami's already established centers, the cheaper. This unconscious, land consuming pattern of development swept the U.S. during the late 20th century but especially so in Miami. Low-density housing spread outwards where the previously impenetrable swampland was now wrung dry.

Leisure

(Hotel)

"Miami...a city without a past, a city based in large part on the artifice and fantasy of resort culture. It was invented wholesale by developers, architects, public officials, residents and tourists - all of whom were committed to the idea of Miami as a city sui generis... Though the city's constructed tropical landscape and architecture could offer no true authenticity, its creation reveals a fundamental mechanism of Miami's modern identity - a search for rootedness in the environment."

-Allan T. Shulman

THE FLAMINGO

The Flamingo Hotel was the first manifestation of Miami's aspiration of leisure to reach Miami Beach. The hotel was developed by Carl Fisher in 1920, between his motorboat speedway in Biscayne Bay and his polo fields that occupied the drained swampland of Miami Beach. The Flamingo's name invoked imagery of the exotic and tropical, despite being designed by architects from Philadelphia. Rejecting the wood vernacular tradition that Flagler's Royal Palm Hotel partook in, the Flamingo looked like it could have been built in Philadelphia, Chicago, New York, or any other major U.S. city. By name and landscaping alone was the hotel dressed for its life in Miami. The Flamingo was just one example of hundreds across the country of what Rem Koolhaas called "The Great Lobotomy" of Architecture. The architectural shell that had nothing to do with its interior activities had arrived in Miami.

The Flamingo Hotel,
(Above) after having its
rooftop dome flung off
in the 1926 hurricane.

Paradise in parcels.
The privatization of the
beach, with separate
access from each hotel
to the Atlantic ocean.

POSTCARDS, A PRIMARY METHOD OF ADVERTISEMENT FOR MIAMI BEACH HOTELS IN THE MID-20TH CENTURY.

PARADISE IN PARCELS

With the rise of the American vacation after the second world war, Miami, especially Miami Beach, was inundated by middle-class families, propelled southward by gasoline and promises of healing sunshine. Hotels, in selling the idea of a "slice of paradise," competed to provide an ideal vacation for the right price. An alternate to the grand hotel experience, Miami's smaller hotels, whether they were on Collins Avenue on the Beach, or back on the mainland near Bayfront Park, all worked to sell a more affordable version of the same thing.

Postcards were a primary method of advertising, and in analyzing these depictions of the hotels, a common aspirational trend can be identified. The hotels were drawn in isolation within a tropical landscape. Almost always depicted as if they were situated between two vacant lots, the postcards, competing to portray their subject in the most flattering light, imply that isolation is the ideal. A private world unto itself, organized on axis with the ocean and surrounded on both sides by a fabricated natural landscape. On one end of the axis, closest to the road, there is the air-conditioned tower. The lobby at the bottom of the tower instantly provides the reprieve from the climate that attracted the visitor in the first place. Past the tower is the pool; clean, private, and exclusive to guests of the hotel. The pool, a sterile and timid fabrication of swimming in the ocean, eliminates the possibility of encountering sea life or sand between the toes. Past the pool is access to the ocean. A controlled, orchestrated entrance to the Atlantic, upon which the visitor has complete personal freedom to access nature as they please. When they are tired by the surf and the sun, they can retreat once again to the private realm of the hotel. In Miami, this amenitization of nature was revolutionized.

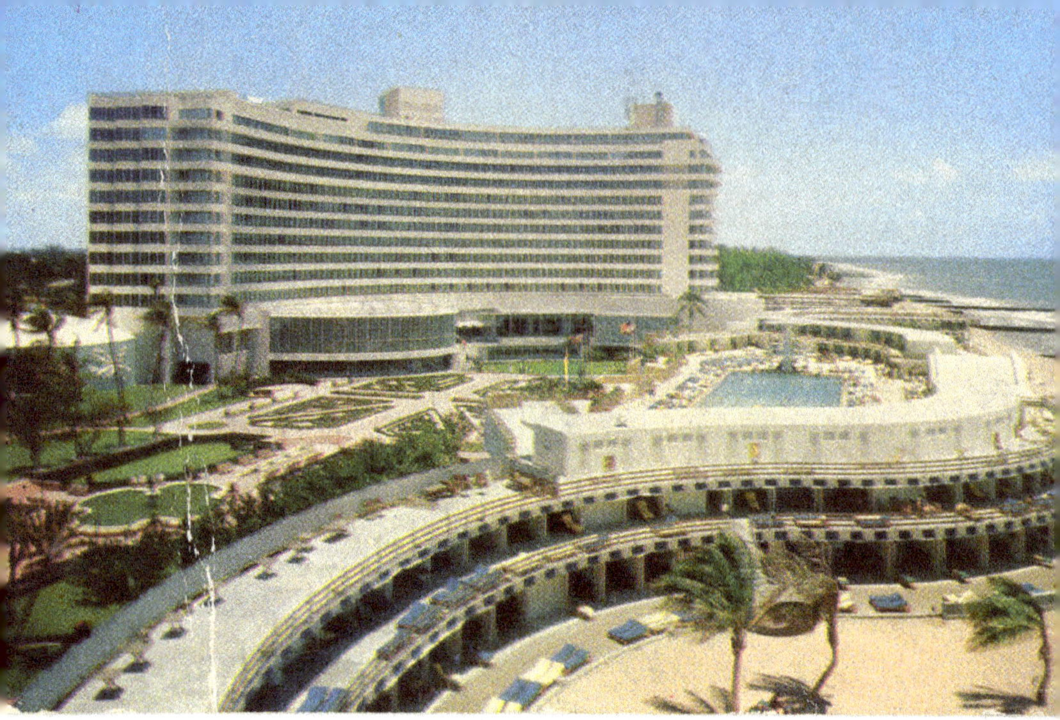

The Fontainebleau, pinnacle of leisure and opulence.

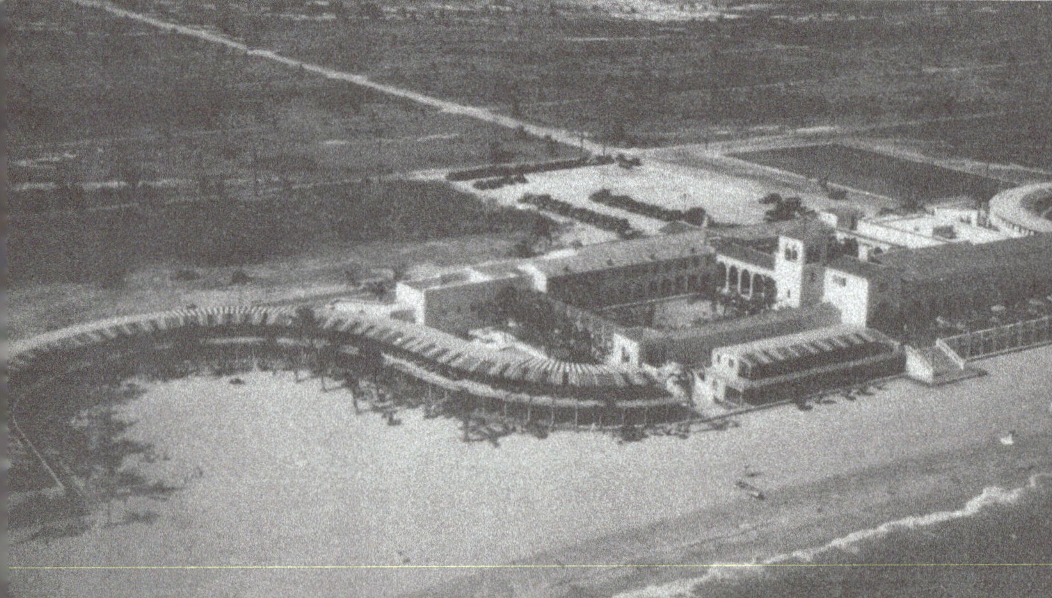

Lapidus' Cabanas took obvious inspiration from the cabanas of the Surf Club, designed by Russell T. Pancoast in 1929.

THE FONTAINEBLEAU

When the Fontainebleau opened in 1954, it represented the peak achievement of hotel opulence. Its lobby alone was 17,000 square feet. Morris Lapidus, the architect of the grand hotel, drew from his extensive background in designing commercial space to create an amenity playground that was unprecedented. One could swim in any of the hotel's three pools in 80 degree Miami weather, and then cool off their sun-tanned skin with a bit of indoor ice skating. The power of the air conditioning in the building was that of legend. Deep within the heart of the structure, a 1,300 ton air-conditioning apparatus kept the building cooled to exact specifications.

The Fontainebleau was developed by hotelier Ben Novack, who had just completed his previous scheme to purchase the land on which the hotel sat. To acquire the land, he partnered with Harry Mufson, and they bought the lot for for $2.3 million. The partnership was fraught with controversy, and ended when Mufson claimed he had been tricked, and Novack was the sole owner on the deed for the land. Novack's pattern of toxic business partnerships would not end with the purchase of the Fontainebleau's plot. Novack was destined to make the Fontainebleau his crowning achievement.

Novack hired Morris Lapidus to design the Fontainebleau, giving him the role of comprehensive designer. It was Lapidus' first solo hotel design. Novack and Lapidus, of course, were both transplants to Miami hailing from New York City. The two would create the most magnificent hotel Miami Beach had yet to see. They would be terrible parents; their constantly quarrelling and bickering would see their child born out of an unhappy partnership. Their creation would, nonetheless, grow up to be one of the most notable hotels in Miami's history, both for its design and its sheer impact on the culture of Miami Beach. The site, situated on Millionaires' Row, was far north of Miami Beach's main hotel hub. The isolation and scale of the hotel allowed it to be a world within itself, simultaneously anti-urban and programmatically intense. Lapidus took full advantage of the hotel's otherworldly site and began to implement his "Architecture of Joy," the name of his manifesto for architecture as instrument of hedonistic pleasure.Unlike the first generation of grand hotels in Miami which included the Royal Palm Hotel, Flamingo Hotel, Nautilus Hotel, and Roney Plaza, the Fontainebleau was born with air conditioning, a new vital organ in the mid 20th century building. This new technology allowed for the building to be less dependent on operable windows and interior breezes. Instead the sweeping facade was adorned with sleek, sealed ribbon windows which gave the building a mechanical rhythm to complement its organic curve. Lapidus dutifully followed Flagler's agenda of tall palms, white sand, and green grass. He included the Royal Palm Hotel's motif of a hard, clean edge between the conquered land and the sea for the Fontainebleau grounds.

Lapidus and Novack's quarrels began when Novack claimed to the the creative originator of the building's design. As later recounted, Novack had called Lapidus after a particularly long session sitting on the toilet, which had inspired Novack. He told Lapidus that he wanted the building he was paying for to be curved in a manner similar to a toilet seat. Though likely true, this conversation alone could not possibly have allowed Novack to claim that the building was his brainchild. By the end of the job, Novack and Lapidus were still fighting as to who had creative authorship of the design. In an attempt to subdue Lapidus, Novack refused him payment for his work, and Lapidus in turn, physically attacked him. *"I was running after him with a three-by-six screaming at the top of my lungs- everything stopped on the job-and saying this man must die," Lapidus later reminisced. "He ran away and I ran after him and it took about three of the partners to restrain me. I blacked out... or I would have flattened him."*

The Spite Wall (Building on the Left.) The building on the right was Constructed on the Eden Roc Property in 2008.

SPITE WALL

The rivalry would not end when the job was over. After the construction of the Fontainebleau was finished, Lapidus was commissioned to design the Eden Roc hotel on the adjacent lot to the north. Novack, annoyed that Lapidus would try to one-up his own design merit on the adjacent lot, decided that it was a perfect time for an expansion to the Fontainebleau. His expansion, however, was less about improving his own site and more about degrading the Eden Roc's. Fontainebleau's North Tower, seventeen stories high, had the practical purpose of doubling the capacity of the hotel. But the real blow to Lapidus was the tower's massive blank facade which faced towards the Eden Roc. No windows, no ornamentation, nothing but unadorned spite.[2]

The proximity of building envelope to the adjoining lot might have been standard in places like New York, Chicago, or other large cities, but in Miami, the clear, warm sky was an unalienable right. This was an act of war. In this battle, Novack had the better ground. His new building, situated on the south side of the Eden Roc, was placed not only with an ugly blank face in extreme proximity to the neighboring parcel, but was also built high enough to block out the sun. A shadow was cast over the Eden Roc's pool. By increasing his number of hotel rooms available, Novack also nullified a major amenity of his competition.

Novack had slighted Lapidus in the battle between the two adjoining parcels. In the war proving design excellence, however, Lapidus had a veritable nuclear arsenal. He would go on to design masterpieces such as the Americana, the Deauville, the Carillon, and dozens more.

THE EDEN ROC, TODAY

SPEED

"Miami is not a large city in the usual sense, but rather a series of experiences accessible in less than ten minutes by car..."
-Maurice Culot

CONGESTION OF THE MACHINES

In Miami, congestion does not refer to warm bodies pressed together, competing for space on the sidewalk. Congestion refers to cold air-conditioned capsules, competing for square footage of asphalt. Though distanced several feet apart, and separated by two layers of glass, motorists feel the same elevated cortisol levels and claustrophobia that their downtown-dwelling forefathers felt when pressed up against each other on foot. Operating private property on public land is thrilling at high speeds, and miserable when moving at a snail's pace. Driving past rows of palms or under the tunnel-like canopies of banyan trees is bliss. Competing for public space in close proximity to others' mobile capsules of air-condioned real estate is hell. When the highways are clear, however, their access ramps offer an exquisite interpretation of the city. Viewed from the highway at 70 miles per hour, the buildings in downtown pirouette and spin in ways impossible to perceive without aid of machine. Architecture of the machine age was nimbler, more dynamic than ever before, at least from the distance and height of the elevated highway.

Belgian architect Caroline Mierop would later write about the driving experience:

"As the road passes through Miami, it acquires a guard of honor made up of thousands of proud, elegant Royal palms. Beyond all this, there is the incredible quality of distance which characterizes the city landscapes. The sea-level causeways linking Miami with Miami Beach and the man-made islands in the

CARS GATHERED BEFORE FORMAL DEVELOPMENT ON CORAL WAY AND PONCE DE LEON BOULEVARD.

THE TRANSFORMATION FROM RESORT TO CITY REQUIRED A HIGHWAY TO UNIFY FLORIDA'S ARCHIPELAGO OF LAND-SPECKLED SEA.

bay, give a unique sense of intimacy with the water... The approach to the city centre via the high-level expressways is equally impressive. After the amphibious car, the flying automobile. The sweeping curves of concrete reveal a changing panorama of downtown..."[1]

THE AUTOMOBILE CENTER OF THE UNIVERSE

Carl Fisher, in connecting his real estate ventures to the North by assembling the Dixie Highway, ensured that Florida would stay at the cutting edge of highway building. It was the age of the petrol pioneer; families were coming southward to Miami in droves. In 1953, legislation was signed to commission The Florida Turnpike, the state's most ambitious highway project to date. The Turnpike cannot be seen as a public works project, but rather a real estate venture by the State. Of course, no Florida real estate scheme could be inaugurated without a massive advertising campaign. The American Automobile Association took part, and over two million pamphlets and maps were circulated across the U.S. The very first year, the toll road did not only break even, but created surplus revenue of three million dollars.[2]

INHERENT AUTO DEPENDENCY

It is widely accepted that Miami's auto-dependency was a result of the post-war urban planning practices that encouraged sprawl across the metropolitan area. However, auto-dependency existed in Miami long before it was enforced by urban design (as seen in the image on the top of the adjacent page). The polycentric nature of the metropolis, combined with its highly speculative real estate prices, led to a grid at the heart of the city that was sparse with development, a departure from the typical pattern characterized by agglomerations of buildings within walkable distances. Miami's highway and city planners took this trend of auto dependency and cast it in stone by paving auto-dependent street networks, but even more permanently, cast it in

...AMI'S GRID PEPPERED WITH DISCONNECTED BUILDINGS, NOT CLUSTERED TOGETHER IN WALKABLE NEIGHBORHOODS.

THE DOLPHIN EXPRESSWAY.

The Downtown Interchange. Photograph by Qiazi Chen.

ownership. In 1961, the Palmetto Expressway was built, creating a new bypass of downtown. The Palmetto facilitated truck traffic to the ranches, farms, and industries that still covered much of the metropolis' land.

TROPICAL FRUITS AND HIGH SPEED

The trucking industry as we think of it today was completely different during the birth of Miami. A trucker in the 1800s was typically a farmer of vegetables. These "truckers" got their name from the French word troquer, meaning "to exchange or barter."[3] The entire American agricultural industry was shaped by the evolution of the farming trucker's route. Even by the early 1900s, most farms were within a day's journey by horse-drawn cart of a town center. However, as large urban populations grew, so did the demand for food. As cities expanded, farmland was pushed further and further away from the city centers. Enabled by refrigeration, the market for fresh produce was no longer a local market, but a regional one. For example, in New York City it was not uncommon to purchase food at a market that was grown in the Carolinas. A race began between the truckers to compete for these hot markets. The farther south one farmed, the earlier their crops could be in season. Produce farmed in the south without competition from northern farms commanded high prices.[4] Not to be beat, northern farmers began to experiment with the centuries-old technology of greenhouses, sometimes with two separate layers of glass, and a constantly burning coal furnace in order to combat the cold. This method was advantageous even for those in the southern United States, as Floridians could grow tropical fruits under glass in the winter, selling them for exorbitant prices. In the winter, pineapples were sold in bulk, before retail markup, at $1.50 apiece.[5]

By 1900, Florida's coasts had great potential, if only they could only obtain fresh goods and ice without having to import them from Savannah.[6] Florida's one true advantage was its climate. Florida's disadvantage was that it was disconnected from the great infrastructure of the Northeast, where the very first American truckers would find the market for their goods. Within the next 30 years, Miami would see hundreds of miles of railway and roadway scraped into its freshly drained swamplands. Miami's new grid of thoroughfares neatly divided plots of private land in a north-south-east-west orientation, quite literally paving the way for the land boom that would see a city rise up out of the marsh. Miami's second wave of auto-centric planning, however, would not be so unanimously productive.

RACISM, FOR EQUALITY'S SAKE

The development of Miami's highways under the premise of benefit of all came with a heavy cost to its underrepresented black community in the early 1960s. To this day, a central tenant of the Florida Department of Transportation's mission statement is providing a transportation network that is "congestion free." In the pursuit of a highway system sparsely populated by motorists, planners fell into the same trap for replanning the highways that Le Corbusier fell into when replanning cities. Both opposed congestion, and in doing so, both opposed success. Trying to eliminate congestion caused by traffic incoming to Miami, the highway and city planners of the day used eminent domain to fulfill their vision of a wide, congestion free highway. The elimination of congestion was one objective, the other much more sinister in character. Originally proposed along an old railroad corridor, local officials saw an opportunity to use the construction of the highway to combat what they deemed urban blight: Overtown. In fact, Overtown, originally called Colored Town[7], was one of the most financially successful black neighborhoods in the entire country between 1920 and 1955. Despite this, in the late 1950s, white city leaders still refused to see the area as successful; they saw it as an area of undesirable people that blocked further expansion of the downtown.

OMINOUSLY TITLED PAMPHLET (FACING PAGE)

we may be
COMING YOUR WAY
W. SANFORD
FLORIDA STATE ROAD DEPARTMENT

WE MAY BE COMING YOUR WAY

Some portions of the proposed North-South Expressway were reorganized because of objections raised by wealthy landowners who felt their riverfront property would lose value if the expressway was built too close, so the highway was replanned and moved farther west. Similar considerations were not made for the residents of Overtown, who were instead handed ominous informational pamphlets, informing them they had the right to three appraisals before the government paid them for their confiscated land. Those who owned land adjacent to the parcels the Florida State Road Department purchased were less lucky. They were not compensated for the decreased value of their land, overshadowed by Miami's newest attraction. To the media, monstrosity represented magnanimity. The highway was advertised cheerily by the New York Times, which likened the project to a Christmas gift to all members of the city. *"It will spread over 20 blocks and climb eight stories into the Miami skyline so that traffic can crisscross at four levels."* The Expressway proved to be just as gargantuan as promised, and ten thousand residents, almost all black, were displaced. Overtown would never regain its national prominence and would descend into decades of neglect.

Construction of the Downtown Interchange and Highway

SPECTACLE

BAY AS SPECTACLE

During the era of the first World War, the United States Navy saw fit to use a small island in the southern side of Biscayne Bay to stage naval aviation. They took this island, and with some dredging and filling, turned it into a peninsula of the mainland. After the war was over, the peninsula was converted for civilian use. It would be named Dinner Key because of the spectators who would bring picnics to watch the planes take off from the water. In January of 1929, Pan-American Airlines would move their center of operations for flights from Key West to Miami. At this time, Pan-Am serviced a single destination: Havana. Within just two years, Pan-Am rapidly expanded and aquired Dinner Key from a competing airline for their own operations. For the era of seaplanes, this would be the nexus of activity. By 1940, Dinner Key was seeing over 160 flight arrivals per day, and began a navigational training academy that was to see over 2,000 graduating aerial navigators per month.

With all of this activity, the Bay itself was a spectacle for the people of Miami. This was nothing new, as people had previously flocked to see giant works of human manipulation of the Bay. In 1903, residents witnessed the inception of the Government Cut, which opened up a shipping channel between Biscayne Bay and the Atlantic Ocean. People gathered around Biscayne to watch John Collins' bridge constructed between the mainland and Miami Beach. People had been gathering to see spectacles in the bay for the entire history of the city. Furthermore, the very act of reconstructing an island into a more regular plan to fit programmatic needs was established at the very founding of the city through Flagler and the hard, clean edges constructed between land and water at his Royal Palm Hotel. This would be a tradition that would continue with the 1920s construction of, as Jean-Francois Lejeune put it, *"lozenge-shaped*

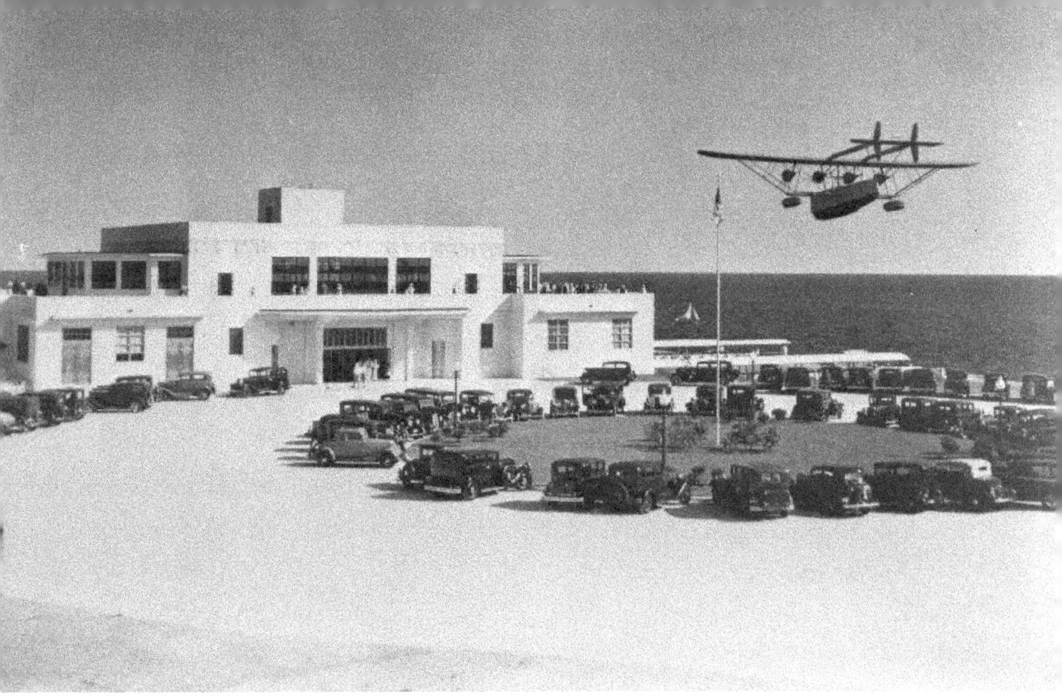

Dinner Key

University of Miami Students partaking in the spectacle of the bay, an unending Atlantean civic drama.

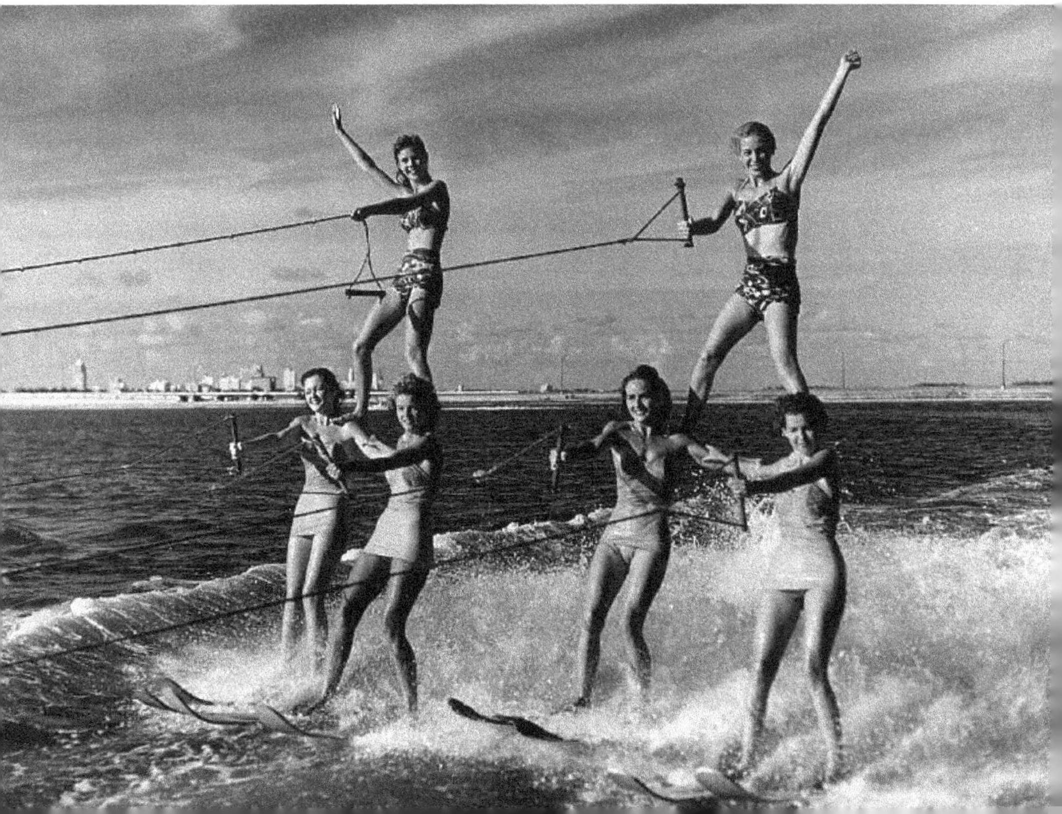

MIAMI MARINE STADIUM. PHOTOGRAPH BY QIAZI CHEN.

forms"[1] of the Venetian, Star, Hibiscus, Palm, and Flagler Memorial Islands.

MIAMI MARINE STADIUM- THE AQUATIC CIRCUS MAXIMUS

Though Interama would never come to be, the spirit behind the fantastic architecture of the proposal was able to manifest itself in the following decades. In contrast to Interama's mostly Anglo-American cast, much of Miami's supertropical architecture was manifested by Latin American architects who came to Miami. Hilario Candela, architect of the Miami Marine Stadium, designed a building that was sensuously constructed from thin-shelled concrete, taking advantage of the concrete craftsmanship and expertise that existed within Miami's construction industry.

In 1962, the City of Miami began to move forward with the idea that Miami should become the boat racing capital of the world. They hired an engineering firm to perform a feasibility study. Unsurprisingly, the firm decided it would be a wonderful endeavor and determined that there was no existing precedent in the world for the boat racing course and facility of the type the Miami City Commission envisioned.[2] The firm, Burke Engineers & Architects, would continue the tradition of the spectacle of the bay through creating geometrically regular shapes out of irregular, naturally formed islands. The watercourse was scraped out of the bay, creating a racing loop that reflected the forms of the Venetian islands, except in negative, as the raceway was to be on the water, and not on land. This produced the design of a 5,300 foot-long stadium, with the Circus Maximus of Rome as its precedent. Beyond racing, provisions for other cultural events and gatherings were not pursued as Interama's own floating amphitheater threatened to absorb all demand for such a project. Though Interama is largely forgotten now, during its design phase the massive project loomed over all other potential developments in the region.[3]

There was a growing theme among Latin American architects of sports facilities and stadiums that explored the aesthetics of poured concrete. Most notable of these, Oscar Niemeyer and Felix Candela, had pioneered the construction of thin-shelled concrete buildings, stretching the material to its technological limits. Felix Candela was in fact a distant cousin of Hilario Candela's, and would influence Hilario's works, including the Miami Marine Stadium. Hilario had not only worked with Felix, but also had met with Luigi Nervi, the European Architect famous for his concrete works of modernist architecture. Once the raceway was completed, Hilario Candela was commissioned to design the grandstand. Completed in 1964, entirely from poured concrete, the structure was constructed in the same spirit that the bay was dredged, just in reverse. Instead of removing muck and oolitic stone, muck was poured in the form of concrete slurry and oolitic stone was added in the form of aggregate. The design called for a dramatically cantilevered roof, structured to give maximum viewing angles to those in the stands. Candela had learned techniques from his fellow architects, such as folding the roof to add vertical structural support, as well as reducing the thickness of the slab as it cantilevered out from its supports. The local structural engineers had no way to calculate the forces that were moving through the roof except by standard, flat designs. Candela had to work with the engineers, who at the end of the day required that additional supports be added, because they couldn't calculate the impact of these design techniques. Hilario Candela would later recount touring the stadium with his distant cousin and fellow architect, Felix Candela. Pointing at the structure, Felix quipped: "You know, those columns are redundant." Hilario grimaced. "I know."

In the end, the stadium was a impressive work of architecture. Seemingly floating, the roof was the defining feature of the project. Major concerts were held at the stadium, and it represented all that Miami saw in the Bay. Biscayne was so important that it needed its own grandstands. The stadium was a nexus of spectacle for over 20 years, until it was damaged in 1992 by Hurricane Andrew. Reports proved the structure was intact but needed repairs, and it has remained closed ever since. Many attempts have been made to reactivate the site, including designs that call for the preservation of the structure, as well as its demolition and redevelopment.

DODGE ISLAND

From 1959 until 1970, Miami developed a new port and ocean terminal complex that was world class, and would prove to be one of the defining infrastructure projects for the city as a whole. The entire island was constructed from fill from the Bay; just like every other project in Miami, something from nothing. Miami's port was previously just north of downtown Miami. Established by the

Flagler and his henchmen in the late 19th and early 20th century, the area was unfit for further growth of the industrial uses, especially as development of the downtown was putting pressure on the prices of lots around this industrial area.

Furthermore, Miami was the nation's leading passenger hub. As early as 1943, Miami's Port was the leading port of entry for the country, with over 45% of all international passenger arrivals and departures through its waters. By the 1950s, the cruise ship industry was set to explode, and the City began to consider proposals for redevelopment or relocation of Miami's port.[4] In 1959, it was finally decided that the new port would be constructed on an entirely new island in Biscayne Bay, called Dodge Island. The island was 270 acres large and constructed completely from sediments dredged from the adjacent channel, simultaneously deepening the lane for large boats. In contrast to most modern ports, Port of Miami's terminal was meant to be seen. To the north of Dodge Island, on the terminal's broad side, the Rickenbacker Causeway offered a clear view of the new, human-made island. To this day, cruise lines construct terminals both to serve their passengers and advertise to peering eyes from passenger-side windows of cars cruising along the Causeway.

The terminal was transparent and aimed to increase visibility both from afar and within the complex. Punctuated by tropical landscaping, including citrus trees, orchids, and palms, the complex welcomed newcomers with an immediate introduction to its fabricated landscape. Within 12 years, the number of cruise ship passengers would explode from just 115,000 in 1959 to 700,000 in 1971.[5]

Proposal for Dodge Island. (Above)

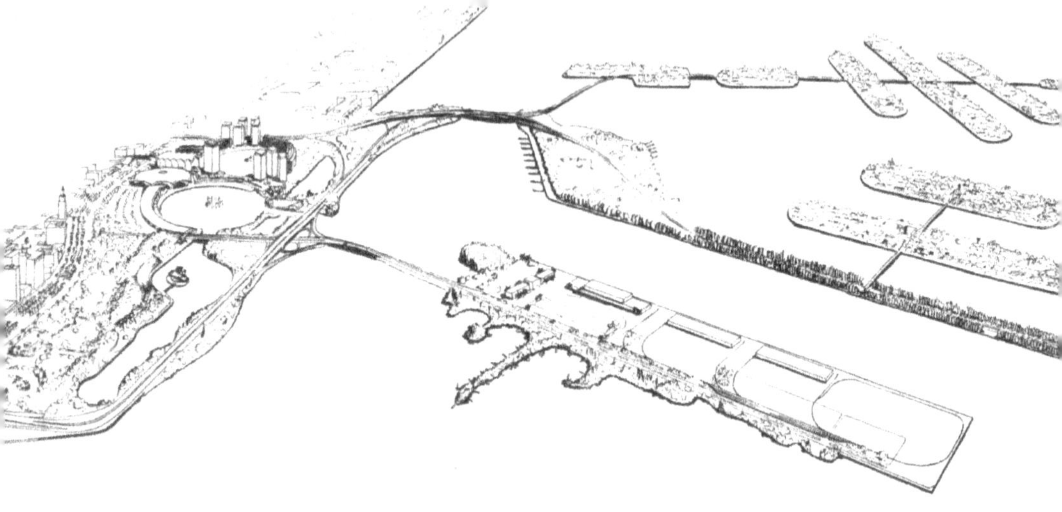

Before Dodge Island's Construction. (Below)

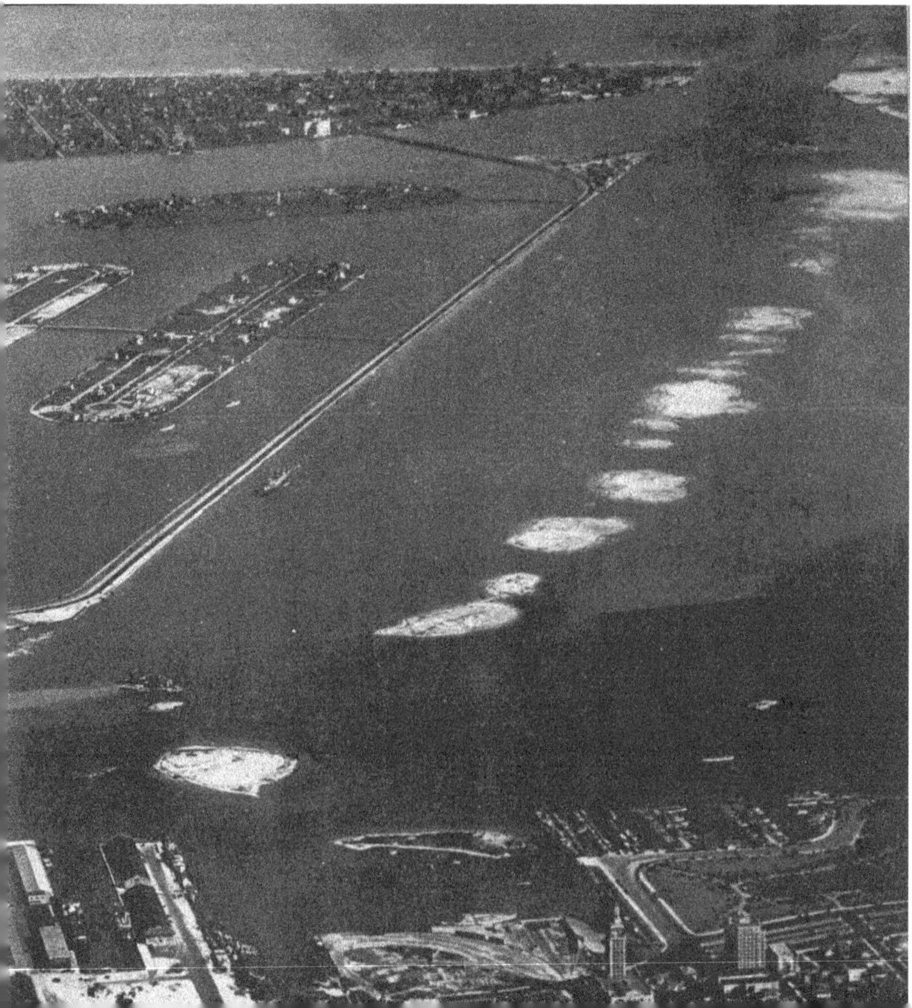

DODGE ISLAND TODAY. PHOTOGRAPH BY QIAZI CHEN. (FACING PAGE)

THE TYRANNY OF BEAUTY

From the world's spotlight in the 1960s as the "American Riviera", Miami Beach would, over the years, lose its special status in American vacation culture. As the average American gained access to jet travel and international destinations, Miami became a stop along the way to more exciting and exotic destinations such as Cuba and the Caribbean. Occupancy was less made up of young tourists staying for a weekend and more comprised of senior citizens living on their pensions. The demographic transition led to the nickname "God's waiting room." This shift left a vacuum of energy in its place. South Miami Beach became quiet and uninteresting. Worse than that, the area fell into the most humiliating situation possible for a Miami neighborhood: an area of inferior financial prospects.

City officials were appalled. Preceded by generations that saw the value of their land multiply one hundredfold, they couldn't bear the shame that came with stagnant real estate prices. However, the planners had an issue... each city block contained around ten individual lots under separate ownership. In the America of the 1970s, there were only two paths towards eminent domain: declare a highway needed to be constructed, or declare the area blighted. Condemn property in the neighborhood, and the state would approve a redevelopment area.

So, in 1975, the city commission boldly declared the area south of Sixth Street as "blighted." The locals were shocked. They had saved their whole lives to retire to a quiet, calm place, and now they were being told that they were an embarrassment to the city of Miami Beach. The Mayor at the time later acknowledged that "It wasn't that blighted. That was just the word we had to use. Some parts of it were bad, but the majority was good. I think we just wanted to change the image. It was becoming a lot of small co-ops for the elderly and we didn't want a retirement community."

The declaration of blight was a self-fulfilling prophecy. The city, anticipating a large redevelopment plan from a private partner, placed a moratorium on building on the entire area. Building owners were barred from making major repairs or improvements. Those running the hotels and apartments saw no reason to fix something that was set to be bulldozed. The buildings began to leak, and the plumbing started to fall apart. Anyone who could afford to sell or move away did. In the end, the city had nothing to show for their act of eminent domain, political indecision and bureaucracy would get in the way of any project being completed. It would take the city nine years to lift the moratorium, leaving in its wake a neighborhood that it turned into a slum. Parallel to the City's disastrous attempts to encourage development were other players in the arena, also attempting to bring back South Beach. Barbara Capitman had very distinct ideas about how she would redefine the area. She and her son would spur a revival in the area that brought back not only the dignity of financial returns to South Beach, but a movement that would put the formerly unglamorous and overlooked area of South Beach on the map. The Capitmans, instead of trying to redevelop the area by making connections through the traditional channels of power and influence, tapped into a new national movement. Historic preservation, though restrictive, was all the rage in the artistic community and amongst the bourgeoisie. Barbara Capitman believed in the tradeoff of complete developmental freedom for the value that comes with identity. Capitman pounded the pavement for years on end in a marketing campaign that relied on grassroots activists, not expensive hired staff.

Barbara Capitman saw something few others saw in the buildings that comprised Miami Beach. The porthole windows, glass block accents, and dramatic spires and fins adorning the buildings were unlike anywhere else. She recognized that the buildings, before the word Art Deco was even used to describe them, had a distinct character. It didn't matter that the area wasn't even comprised mostly of Deco, over half the buildings were expressed with some other aesthetic style, be it Mediterranean Revival, Mission, Moorish, or Florida Vernacular. It didn't matter whether the residents had any emotional attachment to the buildings, many of which were half the retirees' age. Besides, Miami was a place where people went to get away from the past. Miami was about NEW, it was about FRESH. It certainly wasn't about 40-year-old buildings whose pipes were just beginning to get leaky.

To Barbara Capitman, those challenges could be overcome. Reality could be overcome. Capitman sought out and recruited those who were most adept at changing reality: artists. In preparation for the coming campaign, her son bought a handful of hotels that were sleepy, dilapidated, and smelled of that which the city of eternal youth feared most: old age.

Miami's draw is that people can come to the city to reinvent themselves. The Art Deco buildings, too, had the capacity to reinvent themselves, to become new and glamorous like they never had been when they were brand new. If Miami Beach was sleepy, it had the color palette of a fever dream. The buildings could be exactly like some of the retirees who inhabited Miami Beach, those who were active in the community, those who dressed in bright colors that contrasted with their tanned bodies. Nobel laureate Isaac Singer wrote, *"They are so eager to appear young. Perhaps they try to convince themselves that here is the Fountain of Youth, that death will be confused by their clothes."*

Leonard Horowitz moved to Miami Beach after being cut off from his family's fortune when he revealed to his father that he was gay. In 1976, he landed in Miami and headed straight for the beach, working as a doorman during

Leonard Horowitz's Color Palette.

FRIEDMAN'S BAKERY, FEATURED ON THE COVER OF PROGRESSIVE ARCHITECTURE MAGAZINE.

the day. His hobby was painting, and he was known by residents of Miami Beach for riding around the neighborhood on his bicycle. As he explored, he observed the hotels of the historic district. He saw the buildings lining the street, with the paint peeling in hues of white or beige with touches of color used as trim. He began to develop a vision for something much more fantastic. Those colors he saw were used as trim for the buildings that were otherwise bland and unexceptional among the patchwork of different building styles. He took these subtle pastel hues and wove the fabric of the city together in a single palette. This palette, part derived, part invented, complemented the tropical landscape the buildings were situated in: *"golden sand, shell pink, seafoam green, Caribbean blue, sunset orange."*

Horowitz would join Barbara Capitman's Miami Design Preservation League, and his efforts would be essential to the history she was constructing. Capitman, with her close ties to the artist's community, and, just as importantly, the art collector's community, understood one thing. Elegant ballrooms and tea served out of silver pots was no longer "in", and the rich had a new prerogative for what was in style: authenticity. It was authenticity that would make South Miami Beach cool, with its cost-cutting architecture and restrained opulence. The simple hotels took up almost all of their buildings lots, with tight pedestrian walks cutting between. Few had swimming pools, but what they lacked in amenities they attempted to make up for with intimacy, featuring terrazzo floors and fireplaces with unique designs.

Capitman was a master of hyperbole and storytelling. She tracked down newspaper and magazine reporters and tried to get them to write stories about the Art Deco architecture of Miami Beach. It worked. Articles were written internationally about Miami Beach's art scene and the Art Deco buildings in which the scene was active. The neighborhood was back on the map in a big way.

Tirelessly, she pushed not only for social recognition, but for institutional recognition as well. The National Trust for Historic Preservation, established in 1949, was finally becoming a common tool for redevelopment of neighborhoods. If South Beach made it on the National Register for Historic Places, developers would be able to access tax incentives that encouraged rehabilitation, a policy that had passed just months before, in 1976. For years, she vyed for the attention of the National Trust. Capitman and her volunteers at the Miami Design Preservation League understood that the importance they assigned to the neighborhood was anything but by the book when it came to the contemporary attitudes towards preservation. As M. Barron Stofik would later recount in his book, Saving South Beach,

"The required statement of significance barely mentioned the history of Miami Beach except as it related to its architectural development. There was no notice paid to Henry Lum's coconut plantation, John Collin's canal, the city's tawdry gambling days, or any of the thousands of people who made their mark on the city in its sixty-three years of incorporation. It did not claim that the district was rich in history or individual landmarks. Its stated significance was as an architectural time capsule that reflected a particular time, climate, and attitude."

Finally, in 1979, one square mile of South Beach was added to the national register. It was the first twentieth century district to be on the register, and it was one of the largest in the country. Though, on the surface, it would seem as though Miami Beach was the youngest historic district approved, it was actually the oldest. The art deco buildings were not seen by anyone, including Capitman, as being historically important for events that occurred during the buildings' lifetime. Instead, they were approved because they were a Super-

Tropical response to climate. They were approved because of the architectural interpretation of the oldest forces to affect the surface of the earth- sun, water, and land. This was truly a watershed moment for the preservation movement. It would later become widely accepted that architecture could be of historical importance because of the architecture itself, not just the events that occurred within the buildings.

The next year, 1980, Capitman was back in her element. She continued to curate favor within the art world, ignoring the obvious routes to establish social momentum and instead gravitating to where the real influence was. Andy Warhol was in town, with a new exhibition at the Lowe Art Museum in nearby Coral Gables. Capitman took Andy Warhol on a tour of her newly designated district, and he was impressed. It was an important confirmation of what she had known for 10 years. Warhol had a similar nose for the intersection of money and art, and he was onto the same scent.[2]

FORM FOLLOWS FINANCE

"There is always a market for something that has not yet been done."
-Dr. Charles Bohl

FINANCIAL ECSTASY

The land boom of the 1920s is labeled by historians as a time of intense speculation. It is sometimes referred to as the biggest bubble in Florida's real estate history. To call what happened in the 1920s a bubble is a bit of a misnomer, as the term bubble implies that an asset is temporarily at a price that highly exceeds its intrinsic value. For Miami, this situation is the norm, not the outlier. Worthless land has constantly been bought up at ridiculous prices, or at least prices that seem ridiculous until the land sells again at a seemingly even more absurd value. The 1920s were just the beginning of the delirious and absurd history of Miami real estate. After the establishment of the city at the dawn of the 20th century, E.G. Sewell and other speculators found success in campaigning for advertising to northerners. He raised money locally to spend on advertisements in newspapers in the northeast, and the ads proved successful. A massive land rush ensued. As Victor Rainbolt once explained in his book, *The Town That Climate Built,*

"Dealing in real estate became the principal occupation of nine-tenths of the population, the other one-tenth handling it only as a side-line. Prices began to soar, and they have been soaring ever since."

The number of real estate agents became so numerous that they had to wear identification tags at all times in order to prevent accidentally selling to each other. The value of the land became so high, that real estate brokers figured

Downtown Miami during the 1920s land boom.

that they could begin selling the sea, too. Rainbolt went on to describe how far the term "land" could be stretched. *"Sub-divisions stretch from Miami in every direction, even into Biscayne Bay, where "water acreage" has been purchased from the state and islands built and sub-divided, in a far-visioned scheme to match the placid beauty of Venice. Sometimes these "paper islands" are sold before they are built, which shows how far in advance the Miami real estate agent works. He deals in futures. Orders are taken for these "sea lots" and when enough orders are secured to justify the expense he goes out and builds the lots. After selecting his embryonic lot the customer is rowed out to sea and shown the particular wave where his property is located. If there is any dispute the matter is soon washed out."*

In Miami, authenticity isn't inherent; it's constructed. Lots in the bay may be sold before they become land. Miami has always been beyond a "land bubble," because its land is completely fabricated to begin with.

FREE LAND

With the Everglades drained, land value was no longer considered a constraint. Value per acre used to be the measure by which developers looked at a plot of land. The land and the infrastructure to enable it was no longer a factor in the developer's calculations, as the government enabled dry, connected land in unprecedented amounts. Today, the tireless push Westward into the swamp has ceased, and land is no longer a commodity with infinite supply. We are just beginning to see a return to value per acre analysis as the assault on the Everglades winds down. This analysis, when combined with the threat of sea level rise, presents a new way to view Miami's future.

THE NEW HUGH FERRISS

Hugh Ferris changed the world of architecture through his renderings of new zoning codes. By depicting the building envelopes that were allowed under the Manhattan Zoning Code, he paved the way for a new architecture. A parametric architecture, whose creativity comes from that which binds it. Ferriss, in rendering the possible, rather than the buildable, created new meaning for architecture of the city. Almost a hundred years later, a new Hugh Ferriss would emerge.

Joe Minicozzi would graduate with an architectural degree from the University of Miami in 1992. Frustrated with the vapidity of the profession, Minicozzi at a young age became dismayed with architects' angsty need to out-weird each other. Architects were locked in a bidding war for a spotlight in the profession, the only currency accepted was how "different" one's designs could be. During his time in undergraduate studies, he was inspired by an underground University of Miami student organization called SABA: Students Against Bad Architecture. These guerilla design students would sneak around Miami at night and graffiti buildings they deemed especially heinous.

After graduating from the Harvard Graduate School of Design, Minicozzi would find further frustration with the built environment. He saw junk buildings as far as the eye could see in every new suburban development in America. Architects were largely still unconcerned with civic issues, and continued to contrive new problems for themselves without concern for anything outside of the site of their own project. Without communication between sites, there could be no architectural language. Without language, how could buildings be honest?

Instead of contributing to the design of dishonest buildings, Minicozzi preferred the technical and strictly neutral role of planner, curious about how cities shaped themselves through municipal regulations. He became the primary administrator of the form-based code for downtown West Palm Beach, a city that was one of Flagler's original train stops and had a population larger than Miami at one time.

Eventually, he found his frustrations develop into methods of analysis by way of public lectures. He began to tour the country; at first solo, and later backed by an army of analysts who would bring the graphical power of maps to join Minicozzi's verbal arsenal. Effectively an athletic trainer for city planning staff, Minicozzi flies across the country from city to city, performing financial analyses of cities and prescribing dietary plans based on the results.

In encouraging municipalities to plan towards smarter development patterns, mapping is Minicozzi's essential graphic medium. Analytical maps arm Minicozzi like an MRI image arms a doctor. How else is a doctor supposed to suggest something wrong with a patient's body without causing offense? When people can see the tumors in their cities, they are much more likely to sit up straight in their seats and listen. Generally upbeat, but unrelenting in his critiques, Minicozzi shows municipalities maps that illustrate where they are productive and where they are not, and interrogates the findings.

When cities encourage bad architecture and civic spaces, Minicozzi takes delight in revisiting the tactics of the Miami SABA group, but instead of graffiti on buildings, Minicozzi takes buildings on public trial. In his public presentations, he shows poorly designed buildings and public spaces and then points to them on a map. *"Bad design underperforms financially."* Minicozzi might say to the audience. Then he zooms to a map of a larger region, and it becomes apparent to the audience that many iterations of a bad typology act like cancer on a city's ability to see financial returns. *"If you like this building, fine,"* he says coyly. *"But if you want this type of design to be present across your entire city, you better have it written down somewhere that you've made the decision to give up three billion dollars in lost value for your city."*

As Manhattan produced Ferris as its "Skyscraper Theorist," Miami produced Minicozzi to spread its fundamental axiom: Form Follows Finance.

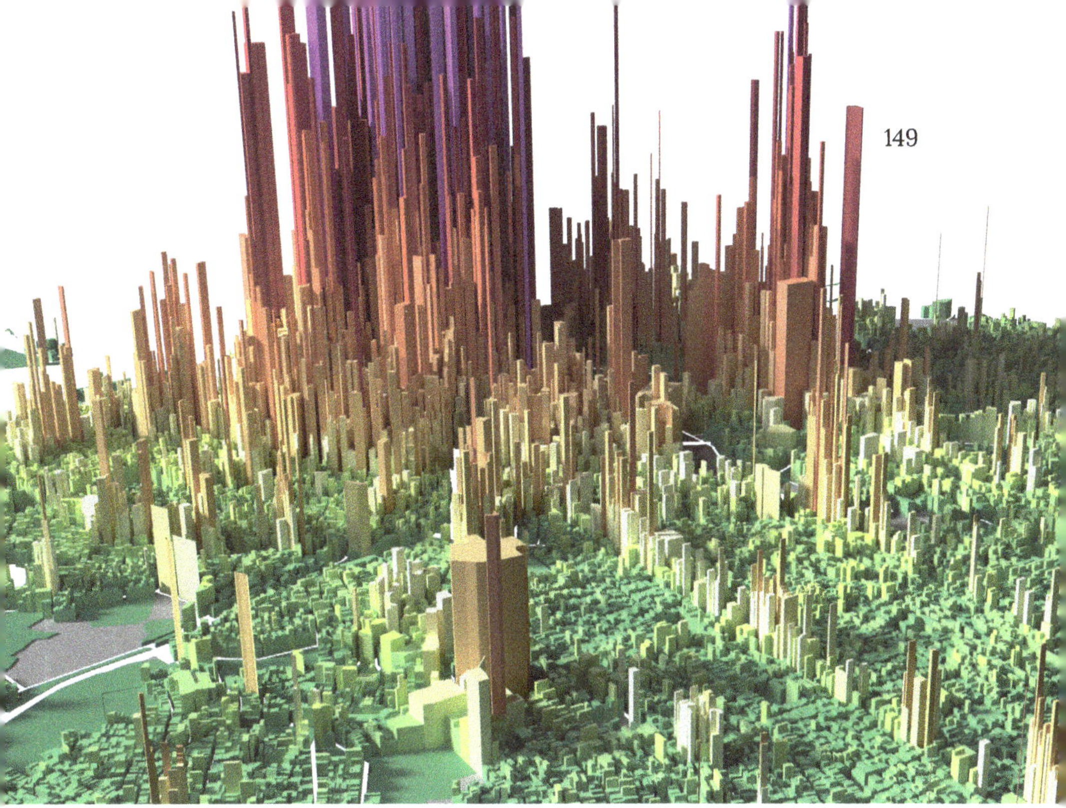

A map of Auckland's value per acre, made by Joe Minicozzi's cartographer Will Creasy.

Hugh Ferriss' renderings of the New York zoning code.

APPENDIX: A SEMI-FICTIONAL CONCLUSION

THE ACHIEVEMENT OF THE SUPER-TROPICAL / THE GREATEST THREAT YET

In the whole of incorporated Miami, less than 5% of the City's land is identified as "Natural" by the architects of its zoning code, Miami 21. Despite this, Miami somehow *feels* as though it is more intimately tied to nature than any other metropolis of its size. Through a combination of its dominant climate, its intimacy with the Atlantic Ocean, and most importantly, the lushness of its fabricated landscape, Miami has become like the nature it has replaced, only more so. Miami has advanced New York's supernatural construction by way of super-tropicalism. As a sort of cruel repayment for this achievement, nature is striking back. Miami sits precariously low in elevation, and this intimacy with the Atlantic means the city that conquered the sea will now have to fight for its life against the rising tides. Venice, Atlantis, and many other Euro-centric city comparisons have been suggested for Miami to reference as examples of how to deal with advancing tides. These comparisons are made in vain. The City of Eternal Youth: vapid, cannibalistic, and beautiful in its brutality, will only ever reference itself.

The world will look to Miami as the city on the front lines, sitting just inches above the rising tides on a drained sponge of a swamp. Miami, sitting on soil that was dumped into the ocean on the promise of making both seller and buyer rich beyond their dreams. Trillions of dollars of desire plowed into freshly fabricated soil. Blood, sweat, and tears of millions, all strangers to the land. A city that is barely a hundred years old. A city for which Hugh Ferriss gave birth in his mind to the ideal architectural form. Ferriss designed three archways to represent those who come and go. The world will be watching with a single question posed to the citizens of Miami:

If all of you are strangers, who will decide to stay?

BRICKELL AND DOWNTOWN MIAMI, LOOKING NORTH. PHOTOGRAPH BY QIAZI CHEN

A MAP, IN THE STYLE OF JOE MINICOZZI'S VALUE PER ACRE, OF MIAMI'S METROPOLITAN REGION.

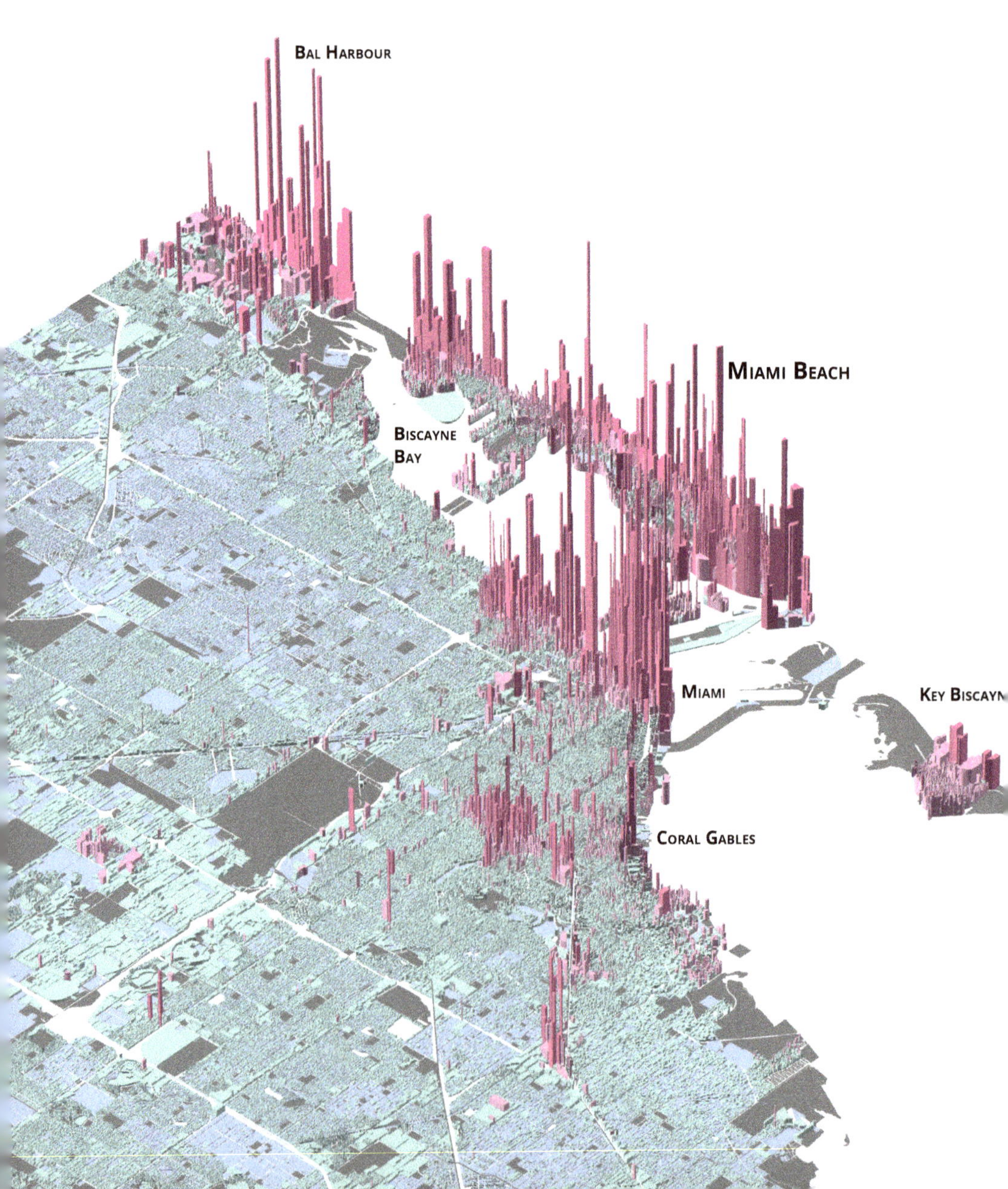

Paradise Lost

Much of Miami's metropolitan region sits just three feet above sea level. Sitting upon calcified coral, Miami's oolitic limestone ground creates a unique problem for the city. Unlike New Orleans or New York, Miami cannot simply dam or levee its way out of the problem of rising tides. The advancing ocean will penetrate the limestone and bubble up from the soil itself. Real estate triage and the decisions to save particular neighborhoods, therefore, not happen as a result of what areas can be protected by sea walls. Instead, valuable land will be saved at a scale much more closely related to the individual lot. This calling to build upwards as the water slowly creeps in is directed to buildings at an individual level. Every lot will live and die by its own decisions, everyone trying to prove their value to justify that they are worth saving. The 21st century will make or break Miami. Selfishness is required to save the city.

Maintaining Investor Confidence

Miami is a city of extreme highs and lows. The darwinistic culture is what gives the city its allure. From the crash of the land boom in the 1920s, to the devastation caused by Hurricane Andrew, Miami is a city of self-reinvention. Miami in its birth rose from the sea; the city has the capacity to adapt to rising tides, so long as its citizens love it hard enough.

Buying The Dip

Throughout the history of Miami, those who bought low and weathered the storm (both financial and literal) have seen their risks pay dividends. The modern investor is unafraid of disaster, for better or for worse, and the phrase BTFD (Buy The Fucking Dip) is now common even amongst the most casual of retail investors. Though high-brow institutions may scoff at this simplistic investment strategy, it has proven profitable for over a century. The scare that will undoubtedly come from the popular realization that Miami will be inundated without adaptation will allow individual investors to buy real estate at affordable prices once again.

Exponential Returns

In 1919, J.E. Ingraham stated that the total taxable property value of the counties alongside the east coast of Florida, from Jacksonville to Miami, was $108 Million. Inflation adjusted, this is $1.6 Billion. This corridor now has a taxable property value of $1.3 Trillion. A modest-sounding growth in value of 9.9% per year has yielded these incredible returns.

City of Eternal Youth

Love of the city from its citizens must be coupled with lust from its investors. The promise of another three-thousandfold return over the next 100 years may be the impetus for Miami's stakeholders to build the infrastructure to prevent the city from becoming this Millennium's first Atlantis. Subjugate nature, or die trying. This was the motto of all the pioneers who became infatuated with the City of Eternal Youth.

THE STORY OF THE POOL, CONTINUED

ACT ONE
EXCERPTS FROM REM KOOLHAAS' DELIRIOUS NEW YORK

*"**MOSCOW, 1923***

At school one day, a student designed a floating swimming pool. Nobody remembered who it was. The idea had been in the air... The floating pool - an enclave of purity in contaminated surroundings - seemed a first step, modest yet radical, in a gradual program of improving the world through architecture. To prove the strength of the idea, the architecture students decided to build a prototype in their spare time...

Due to the chronic Soviet labor shortage, the architects/builders were also the lifeguards. One day they discovered that if they swam in unison - in regular synchronized laps from one end of the pool to the other - the pool would begin to move slowly in the opposite direction... In a secret meeting, the architects/ lifeguards decided to use the pool as a method of auto-propulsion, they could go anywhere in the world where there was water. It was only logical that they wanted to go to America, especially New York...

NEW YORK, 1976

After four decades of crossing the Atlantic, their swimsuits had almost disintegrated...

When the pool docked near Wall Street, the architects/swimmers/lifeguards were shocked at the uniformity (dress, behavior) of their visitors, who swamped the craft in a brute rush through the lockers and showers, completely ignoring the instructions of the superintendents.

Had communism reached America while they were crossing the Atlantic? They wondered in horror. This was exactly what they had swum all this time to avoid, this crudeness, lack of individuality, which did not even disappear when all the businessmen stepped out of their Brooks Brothers suits.

3 MONTHS LATER

Looking at the starry sky reflected in the narrow rectangle of their pool, one architect/lifeguard, still dripping wet from the last lap, answered for all of them: "We just went from Moscow to New York...." Then they dove into the water to assume their familiar formation."

ACT TWO

UNAUTHORIZED SEQUEL

CUBA, 1977

After departing from the shores of New York, the Soviet architects traveled South. As they had to look the opposite way in which they traveled, they looked at the North Star as they swam along the Atlantic Coast of the United States. They arrived, abruptly, on the shores of Cuba, along the Bay of Pigs. Seeing the arrival of a boat on the shores of the bay, and fearing another attack by the United States, the communist Cuban armed forces immediately captured the architects, almost eliminating any chance of Manhattanism from arriving on the island. However, the Architects were allowed to speak of their motherland before their death, so long as their remarks were completely positive. They spoke of the beauty of the concrete brutalist buildings in Soviet Russia. They spoke of the weight and power and conviction they conveyed. As they spoke, the architects thought privately to themselves how ironic it was that despite all the buildings did to aesthetically express courage and strength, what they housed were some of the most anxious and dysfunctional of human organizations. The Cuban officials heard the words of the architects, and, after the they were publicly executed, the officials convened to meet about what they had heard. They decided to erect their newest monuments and public buildings in this brutalist style. Years went by, and the swimming pool in which the long-dead architects landed was still beached on the shore. Many of the discontented Cuban citizens saw the pool, and thought quietly to themselves that it could be put to use and help them escape to the United States.

3 YEARS LATER

One moonless night, many families and individuals decided that it was time to flee. Five separately organized parties that sought to escape with the pool at midnight came upon the craft at the same time, and froze. They looked at each other, and understood that they were all there for the same reason that night. These Balseros then took the craft and, looking towards the shore of their previous homeland, began to swim.

MIAMI, 1980

When they ran aground in the shallow waters of Biscayne Bay, the Balseros realized that they had missed the city's port. The downtown was a few miles north. They shrugged their shoulders, said their goodbyes, and dispersed. Within hours, they had set on their paths, some urban, some rural. Many passed by the Atlantis condominium tower as it was under constuction. A crane was in the midst of hoisting the great palm tree into the square cutout of preserved sky. Upon seeing the palm suspended in the sky, they felt a semi-conscious burst of pride and belonging to the city. Miami welcomed them, not with open arms, but with the cold, impartial promise that they could have a throne of their own if they too conquered the land.

Endnotes

Before the Days of Sub-divisions
1. T.D. Allman. Finding Florida, 19. Grove Press, 2013.
2. T.D. Allman. Finding Florida, 7. Grove Press, 2013.
3. T.D. Allman. Finding Florida, 9. Grove Press, 2013.
4. HistoryMiami Museum. The European Contact Period. March 1, 2019. Exhibition.
5. HistoryMiami Museum. The European Contact Period. March 1, 2019. Exhibition.
6. John Sewell. Miami Memoirs, 177. Arva Parks & Co, 1987.

Subjugate, Then Integrate
1. John Rothchild. Up for Grabs, 27. University Press of Florida, n.d.
2. John Rothchild. Up for Grabs, 25. University Press of Florida, n.d.
3. John Rothchild. Up for Grabs, 30. University Press of Florida, n.d.
4. Allan T. Shulman. "Malling Lincoln Road." In Miami Modern Metropolis, 234.
Bass Museum of Art, n.d.

Guavanormativity and the True Origins of the Sealed Building
1. Daniel Fernandez Pascual, and Alon Schwabe. "Banananormativity, Transplants, and the Genetically Eroded." In The Empire Remains Shop / Cooking Sections. Columbia University Press, 2018. empireremains.net.
2.Arva Moore Parks. George Merrick: Son of the South Wind, 68. University Press of Florida, 2015.
3. T.D. Allman. Finding Florida, 32. Grove Press, 2013.
4. Duncan Leatherdale. 2016. "Bananas On The Brink". BBC News. https://www.bbc.com/news/uk-england-35131751.

Coconuts and Concrete: How to Multiply the Land
1. https://flaglermuseum.us/history/flagler-biography
2. David Leon Chandler (1986). Henry Flagler: The Astonishing Life and Times of the Visionary Robber Baron who Founded Florida. New York: Macmillan Publishing Company.
3. Miami Memoirs, Page 61 - Speech of Mr. J.E. Ingraham, Vice-President of the Florida East Coast Railroad, Before the Women's Club, November 12, 1920
4. Victor Rainbolt. The Town Climate Built, 127. Miami, Fla: Parker Art Printing Association, 1924.
5. T.D. Allman. Finding Florida, 319. Grove Press, 2013.
6. Miami Memoirs, Page 61 - Speech of Mr. J.E. Ingraham, Vice-President of the Florida East Coast Railroad, Before the Women's Club,

November 12, 1920
7. T.D. Allman. Finding Florida, 320. Grove Press, 2013.
8. John Sewell. Miami Memoirs, 150. Arva Parks & Co, 1987.
9. Ibid, 145.
10. Ibid, 150.
11. Ibid, 146
12. Ibid, 161
13. Ibid, 159
14. Ibid, 159

ECOLOGICAL SUCCESSION AND THE PIONEERING SPIRIT

1. Arva Moore Parks. George Merrick: Son of the South Wind, 72-73. University Press of Florida, 2015.
2. Ibid, 72-73.
3. Ibid, 55.
4. Ibid, 62.
5. Ibid, 67.
6. Ibid, 70.
7. HistoryMiami Museum. Coral Gables. March 1, 2019. Exhibition.
8. Della Heiman. Interview with Author, February 11, 2019.

INTERAMA: THE TRUEST MIAMI HAS (N)EVER BEEN

1. Jean-Francois Lejeune. "City Without Memory: Planning the Spectacle of Greater Miami." In Miami Modern Metropolis, 36. Bass Museum of Art, n.d.
2. Ibid.
3. Michael Hoover. "Before Disney Arrived: Florida's Ill-Fated Attempt to Build INTERAMA." The Florida Historical Quarterly, vol. 86, no. 4, 2008, pp. 445–469. JSTOR, www.jstor.org/stable/25594647., Page 446
4. Jean-Francois Lejeune. "City Without Memory: Planning the Spectacle of Greater Miami." In Miami Modern Metropolis, 51. Bass Museum of Art, n.d.
5. Hugh Ferriss. The Power of Buildings: 1920-1950 A Master Draftsman's Record, Project 45
6. Michael Hoover. "Before Disney Arrived: Florida's Ill-Fated Attempt to Build INTERAMA." The Florida Historical Quarterly, vol. 86, no. 4, 2008, pp. 445–469. JSTOR, www.jstor.org/stable/25594647, 449.
7. Ibid, 451
8. Ibid, 453
9. T.D. Allman. Finding Florida, 378. Grove Press, 2013.
12. Ibid, 461.

WEALTH

1. Edna Buchanan, Interview for "Cocaine Cowboys", Directed by Billy Corben
2. T.D. Allman. Miami, City of the Future, 32. The Atlantic Monthly Press, 1987.

Leisure

1. T.D. Allman. Miami, City of the Future, 255. The Atlantic Monthly Press, 1987.
2. Ibid, 256.

Speed

1. Caroline Mierop. "Transatlantic." In Miami: Architecture of the Tropics. New York: Princeton Architectural Press, 1993.
2. Kara Wood. "Highways: The Choreography of Expansion." In Miami Modern Metropolis, 167. Bass Museum of Art, n.d.
3. Dianne Perrier. Onramps and Overpasses, 134. University Press of Florida, 2009.
4. Ibid, 136.
5. Ibid, 139.
6. Ibid, 138.
7. HistoryMiami Museum. Overtown. March 1, 2019. Exhibition.

Spectacle

1. Jean-Francois Lejeune. "Miami's Marine Stadium." In Miami Modern Metropolis, 353. Bass Museum of Art, n.d.
2. Ibid, 353. Bass Museum of Art, n.d.
3. Ibid, 354.
4. Alan Shulman. "Port and Passenger Terminals: Infrastructure as Spectacle."
In Miami Modern Metropolis, 153. Bass Museum of Art, n.d.
5. Ibid, 155.

The Tyranny of Beauty

1. M. Barron Stofik. Saving South Beach. University Press of Florida, 2005.
2. T.D. Allman. Finding Florida, 414. Grove Press, 2013.

Form Follows Finance

1. Victor Rainbolt. The Town Climate Built, 37. Miami, Fla: Parker Art Printing   Association, 1924.

Typefaces:

Lora
Open Sans (small caps, bold)

Illustration Credits

Archival Research:
University of Miami Digital Archives: 12, 23, 25, 27, 33, 35, 101, 103, 104, 109, 115, 121
University of Miami Physical Archives: 47, 102, 106, 119, 126, 137
HistoryMiami Museum, Miami: 69, 71, 73, 75, 85, 86, 87
HistoryMiami Museum - Interama Exhibition by Jean Francois Lejeune and Allan Shulman: 81, 89
State Archives of Florida: 48, 76, 89, 119 (bottom,)
Clum Postcard Collection: 39
FIU Digital Collections: 19
Bass Museum of Art, Miami: 29
Lindley Library, Lindley: 37 (top)
Victoria and Albert Museum, London: 37 (bottom)
J. J. Cade - The Cyclopaedia of American biography, 1918 {{PD-US-expired}}: 42

Corporations:
Duany Plater-Zyberk and Co.: 59
Urban3: 141
Studio Miami: 61, 63

Individuals:
Qiazi Chen: 54(top,) 90, 93, 99, 116, 122, 127, 143
Images by Author: 31, 48 (bottom,) 54 (bottom,) 59 (top,) 97, 111, 131, 144

Misc.:
Princeton Architectural Press: 75
Miami Daily News, 1953: 77
Hugh Ferriss, 1955: 77
The Florida Architect, February 1956: 88
Historic American Building Survey: 121
Planning Review Report of the Miami Seaport Location, 1959: 126 (top)
Progressive Architecture, November 1982: 132
Hugh Ferriss, 1916: 141